Mumbai

Text by David Abram
Photography by Abe Nowitz
Design: Roger Williams
Series Editor: Tony Halliday

Berlitz®

POCKET
GUIDE

Mumbai

First Edition 2006

PHOTOGRAPHY CREDITS
All pictures by Abe Nowitz, except Mary Evans
Picture Library 17; The British Library/
Heritage Archive 18; HIP/The British Library/
TopFoto 19; TopFoto 21; Bridgeman Art
Library 35; Corbis 85, 86; Dinodia 94
Cover photograph: Walter Bibikow/
Jon Arnold Images

CONTACTING THE EDITORS
Every effort has been made to provide accurate
information in this publication, but changes are
inevitable. The publisher cannot be responsible
for any resulting loss, inconvenience or injury.
We would appreciate it if readers would call
our attention to any errors or outdated
information by contacting Berlitz Publishing,
PO Box 7910, London SE1 1WE, England.
Fax: (44) 20 7403 0290;
e-mail: berlitz@apaguide.co.uk
www.berlitzpublishing.com

All Rights Reserved

© 2006 Apa Publications GmbH & Co.
Verlag KG, Singapore Branch, Singapore

*Printed in Singapore by Insight Print
Services (Pte) Ltd, 38 Joo Koon Road,
Singapore 628990.
Tel: (65) 6865-1600. Fax: (65) 6861-6438*

*Berlitz Trademark Reg. U.S. Patent Office
and other countries. Marca Registrada*

Mumbaikars
descend in
droves on
Chowpatty
Beach
(page 48)

CST – formerly
Victoria Terminus
(page 43) – is the
pinnacle of
grandiloquent
Raj-era architecture

The 7th-century
cave temple
on Elephanta
Island (page 67)
has some of
India's finest
ancient
sculpture

TOP TEN ATTRACTIONS

Haji Ali's tomb, the revered Muslim shrine (page 53), is connected to the shore via a causeway ▼

Dawn, when the trawlers are unloading, is the best time to visit clamorous Sassoon Docks (page 31) ◀

Along with the famous Taj Mahal Palace and Tower Hotel, the Gateway of India is Mumbai's defining landmark (page 28) ▶

The cave complex at Ellora is among the world's greatest archaeological treasures (page 75) ▼

A visit to the cinema for a Bollywood movie provides the definitive *'filmi'* experience (page 83) ◀

The central bazaars (page 54): Mumbai at its most compelling ▶

The Chhatrapati Shivaji Museum (page 33) displays treasures from across India ▶

CONTENTS

A ➤ in the text denotes a highly recommended sight

Fact Sheets

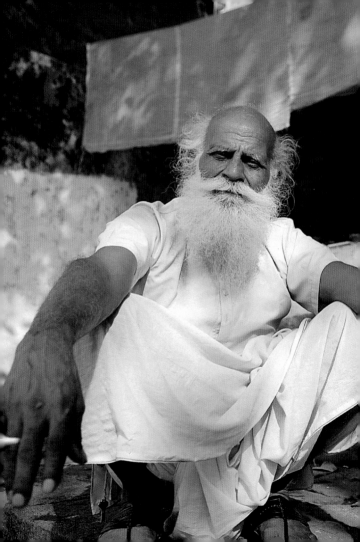

INTRODUCTION

Mumbai – known until 1996 by its former British name, Bombay – is a city of superlatives. Packed onto a narrow spit of reclaimed land that curls like a drooping finger from the Maharashtran coast, it's the world's largest urban sprawl, with a population of 15 million and rising – the most crowded, powerful, corrupt, crime-ridden and compelling metropolis in India. Nowhere else in the country looms as large in the popular imagination, nor exerts such far-reaching influence. Its media images, beamed into countless homes and cinemas across Asia, are lapped up by tens of millions each day.

Under the city's spell, around 500 new arrivals pour daily though the mammoth Raj-era railway stations of downtown Mumbai in search of a better life. Few ever find what they came for, but fewer still return home. For while a squalid slum hut or pavement slab might be their lot today, the 'City of Dreams' – with its glittering film stars, skyscrapers, luxury car showrooms and shopping malls – perennially fuels hopes of a better future.

From the time the East India Company rented its scattered islets from King Charles II for the princely sum of £10 per month – 'to be paid in Gold' – money-making has always been Mumbai's *raison d'être*. And for all the hardship manifest on its streets, there's plenty to go around. Despite holding only 1.5 percent of India's total population, the city generates one third of its tax revenues and 60 percent of its customs duty, with half of the country's maritime trade passing through its port.

Whether dealing in opium, tea, cotton, polished diamonds, info-tech or call-centre support, Mumbai's commercial hub – home of India's stock exchange and the head offices of its largest corporations – has always served as the country's gateway with the West. If something new arrives in India, it will be embraced in this city first – invariably with great gusto and ostentation. Train travel, moving pictures, passenger flight and cable TV all started their subcontinental journeys here in Mumbai, and 'innovation' remains the main watchword.

'City of Sin'

Along with the new commodities and technologies, the prosperous elite who've profited most from them have always been equally eager to experiment with new ideas and lifestyles. As a result, Mumbai has long been India's most Westernised and liberal city, with norms that scandalise more traditional parts of the country. Middle-class Bombay girls date and go to discos, drink draught beer on café terraces in Colaba and party just as hard as their non-resident Indian (NRI) cousins in Southall or Massachusetts. The city also has the closest thing in India to a bona-fide nightlife, with hip clubs and India's only 'out' gay scene.

The other great source of wealth and pride in Mumbai is its record-breaking film business. 'Bollywood' is India's all-conquering dream factory, turning out hundreds of lurid wish-fulfilment musicals each year. Packed with action, romance, melodrama, song and dance, Hindi movies play to 14 million or more cinema goers each day across India, making gods and goddesses of their stars and billionaires of their producers and distributors. The city itself also plays a starring role as the

The earliest known inhabitants of Bombay were a caste of fisherfolk who are thought to have migrated here from the coast of Gujarat in prehistoric times. The Koli still occupy shrinking patches of beach in the south of the city.

On set in Bollywood

backdrop for many of the blockbusters. As a consequence, its landmarks and beaches, grandiloquent Raj-era architecture, black-and-yellow taxis and double deckers have become as familiar to *'filmi'* fans all over South Asia as the Statue of Liberty is to people in the English-speaking world.

What the Hindi movies rarely feature, however, are the downside of the city's glitz and glamour. Although only 30km (19 miles) from north to south, its population is exploding exponentially. An acute lack of space to live and work, dirty air and water, an over-burdened public transport system, sky-high property prices and a decaying infrastructure are just some of the everyday problems faced by Mumbaikars. Add to the equation a fiercely uncomfortable climate, with humidity levels over 80 percent and maximum temperatures averaging 32°C (90°F) for much of the year, and you'll understand why the novelist Aldous Huxley famously described the city of Bombay as 'the most appalling in either hemisphere'.

'City of Gold'

Given how populous modern Mumbai has become, it is astonishing to think that the city was, until a little under 350 years ago, no more than a fishing settlement, remote from the mainstream of late-medieval India. The British were the first to exploit the potential of its magnificent harbour, after King Charles II inherited the seven scattered islands around it through the dowry of Catherine of Braganza in 1662.

By the end of the next century, the colony had eclipsed the East India Company's regional headquarters further north at Surat, and following the cotton boom of the 1860s, along with the advent of steam ships and the Suez Canal, Bombay eventually took over Calcutta's mantle as *Urbis Prima* in India – a title it has never relinquished.

Gateway of India

Behind the city's meteoric rise has always been the diligence and adaptability of its many immigrant communities, drawn from nearly every region of India. Back in the colony's infancy, its first governor, Gerald Augnier, enticed the traders and labour force that he needed to construct the city, 'which by God's assistance is intended to be built', with promises of religious freedom. Among the first to take advantage of the tolerant regime and financial opportunities were the Zoroastrians, or 'Parsis', who had originally come to India in the 7th century AD feeling persecution in Persia. The Parsis were quick to adapt to the new economic climate and soon made themselves indispensable as middlemen between the native population and their European rulers. Many amassed fortunes as shipbuilders, bankers, land reclaimers and industrialists.

Votive offerings at Banganga

Other castes came and flourished too: from Gujarati Jains, to Sindhi Muslims, Punjabi Sikhs, Maratha smiths and clerks, Goan Catholics, Chinese silk traders, and Armenian and Jewish refugees from the Ottoman Empire. Rather than mix in a giant melting pot, however, each of these separate communities congregated in particular districts instead, and to a large extent these ethnic divisions have provided the blueprint for later expansion.

Ethnic Strife

Communal tension, on the other hand, had always been a rarity. Not until the 1970s and 1980s, with the emergence of the pro-Hindu, pro-Maharashtran Shiv Sena party, did ethnic strife rear its ugly head in Mumbai. The Sena and its leader Bal Thackery rose to power by exploiting dissatisfaction among the Marathi-speaking working classes. Gujarati immigrants were the first scapegoats, followed by south Indians and eventually Muslims. Later, in December 1992, it was the Sena who orchestrated the dreadful riots in which 1,400 (mostly Muslims) died. A series of devastating bomb blasts three months later was the response of the

Few places on earth cram such diversity into so compact an area

city's Muslim ganglords to the massacres. Over 300 people were killed in the explosions and several of Mumbai's key landmarks were destroyed.

Since then, an unholy alliance of corrupt politicians, mafia *bhais* (godfathers) and petty gangsters has been holding much of the city and its economy to ransom. Coming in the wake of the terror of 1992–3, such all-pervasive organised crime, affecting everyone from movie moguls to humble slum dwellers, might have crippled many less vigorous cities. But somehow, in spite of the overcrowding, pollution, poverty and corruption, Mumbai continues to flourish like no other city in South Asia.

Exploring the City

Arriving here for the first time, the sheer scale of Mumbai can feel overwhelming. But given a few days, you'll find that the extraordinary vitality of its streets begins to feel less intimidating and more compelling. Few places on earth cram such diversity into so compact an area, and learning to differentiate between the various pieces that make up the constantly evolving cultural mosaic definitely holds its own appeal. Formal attractions such as monuments and museums have their place (not least the wondrous rock-cut cave complex of Elephanta, on an island in Mumbai harbour), but the real fascination for visitors to India's most dynamic city definitely lies at street level: mingling with the crowds in the railway stations at rush hour; wandering the Victorian-era backstreets in search of Irani bakeries, Mangalorean fish restaurants or Gujarati *thali* joints; munching *bhel puri* with the sunset strollers on Chowpatty Beach; watching the cricketers in their dapper whites on the maidans; or exploring the endless markets in the city's heart.

Bombay or Mumbai?

In January 1996, Bombay's name was changed by the right-wing, Shiv Sena-led Municipal Corporation to 'Mumbai'. At the time, the new appellation, derived from the name of the Hindu goddess Mumba-Devi whose temple still stands in the bazaar district, was claimed to be the Marathi name for the island on which the colonial city was originally founded. In fact, it was nothing of the kind: etymologists are agreed that the English word 'Bombay' came from the Portuguese 'Bom Bahia', literally 'Good Bay', which is what the first Lusitanian explorers to come here in 1508 called the harbour where they dropped anchor.

The rebranding exercise was only a part of a broader campaign by the Shiv Sena to replace obviously British or colonial names with more Maharashtran ones. Other victims of the linguistic purge were Victoria Terminus, Prince of Wales Museum and Sahar airport – all renamed after the Maratha warlord, Chhatrapati Shivaji.

A BRIEF HISTORY

Mumbai, or Bombay as it was known until 1996, has always been a city more focused on its future than its past. Scant regard over the centuries has tended to be paid to the remnants of previous eras, but contrary to appearances, ancient settlements and cities did once flourish on the Konkan coast around the archipelago of islands that would later be colonised by Europeans.

Inscriptions found at the Hindu cave temple on Elephanta Island, for instance, record that it was once attached to a major port, Gherapuri, while Buddhist caves carved out of the mountains on the mainland opposite attest to the existence in the area of a highly stratified, orderly society as far back as the 2nd century AD.

Sculptures at Elephanta, used by early Portuguese for target practice

Arab and Portuguese Rule

Other than a body of vague myth, and a couple of temples that may or may not have occupied their present site since ancient times, very few traces of the kingdoms that ruled this remote stretch of coast have survived from the years after the carving out of the caves on Elephanta. Not until 1313, when the Yadava-Maratha ruler, King Bhima, founded a Hindu capital on an island he called Mahikawati (the present-day district of Mahim), do Bombay's islands re-enter the history books. Bhima had fled to the Konkan to escape annihilation at the hands of the Khilji Sultanate of Delhi. But his rule succumbed only a century later to attacks by the Arab Sultan of Gujarat and, in the late 15th century, Mahmud 'Beghada' ('Two-Forts') Shah annexed Vasai (Bassein, 70km/43 miles north of the modern city), along with the scattering of islands to its south, which he named 'Al Omanis'.

It was at these islands that the first Portuguese to probe the northern Konkan arrived in 1508. They called the splendid harbour where they anchored 'Bom Bahia', or 'Good Bay'– the name which, despite Hindu nationalists' claims to the contrary, almost certainly lies at the root of 'Bombay' *(see page 13)*. Not until 1534, did the Portuguese gain a real foothold in the region, however, this time further north at the Gujarati fort of Vasai (or Bassein). The bastion, which they were to rechristen Baçaim, had been ceded to them by the Gujarati sultans after the battle of Daman, and within a couple of decades the Franciscan and Jesuit orders had erected churches, monasteries, a mint and seminary inside its walls.

East India Company

Exactly who owned the thriving little Portuguese town at Baçaim was a moot point when the islands to its south were bundled (along with Algiers) into the dowry of Catherine of Braganza at her marriage to King Charles II of England in

1662. After an ill-fated attempt to install a garrison on the largest of these, the Crown transferred the territory by letter of patent to the East India Company in exchange for a loan of £50,000 and rent of '£10 per month, to be paid in Gold, on the 30th Sept, yearly, for ever…'. No one could have foreseen what a bargain this acquisition would turn out to be.

However, the Portuguese Viceroy of Goa did regard the loss as a shot in the foot for his country's colonial ambitions. In 1668, the year the EIC took full possession of the land, he wrote angrily to Lisbon that 'India will be lost on the same day on which the English nation is settled in Bom Bahia'.

At this time, the EIC's commerce in the region was channelled through the Gujarati port of Surat, 250km (155 miles) north. But the trade was constantly being hampered by interference from the Moghuls and Maratha attacks, eventually forcing the then governor, Gerald Augnier, to shift his headquarters to Bombay, where he set about laying the foundations of 'the city which by God's assistance is intended to be built'.

The *palacio* of a Portuguese nobleman who lived on the island, Garcia da Horta, was converted into the nucleus of Fort St George (in honour of the EIC stronghold on the east coast, later to become Madras). Docks, a mint, a court of justice and a militia were other legacies of Augnier's short but seminal tenure. He also solicited merchant communities from other regions of western India – notably the Parsis and Gujarati Banias – to settle in the new colony, with promises of religious freedom.

> **Garcia da Horta, owner of the manor house around which Fort St George was constructed, was a Jewish convert to Christianity who fled to the Indies in 1534 to escape the Inquisition. A former university professor and physician to the King of Portugal, he was among the first Europeans to research Oriental medicine.**

Disease and Decline

After this upbeat start at the end of the 17th century, Bombay lurched into a sharp decline. Surrounded by marshland, the site and its climate were notoriously unhealthy; there was little good drinking water and 'pestilential vapours' drifted off the tidal flats. Soldiers and EIC recruits, who arrived after 12 months at sea hoping to find their fortunes in the Indies, instead provided fodder for the insatiable 'cormorant paunch' of Mendham's Point cemetery, dying of fevers, 'fluxes', beri-beri and the dreaded 'Chinese death' (cholera). 'Two monsoons are the age of a man,' declared Chaplain Ovington at the time – a prognosis that would become legendary in the annals of British Bombay.

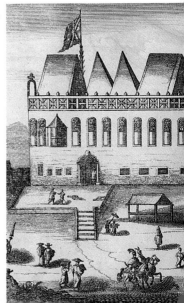

The English Fort of Bombay, 1671

Faced with the prospect of an early grave, many found solace in debauchery, and records of life for the colony's wretched inhabitants at this time are filled with accounts of drunkenness, gluttony and fornication.

Constant attacks made by Sidi pirates and the troublesome Marathas proved to be additional perils. A Moghul-backed siege then eventually drove away around half of Bombay's population in 1690, leaving behind what one observer described as 'only…broken traders and renegade seamen'.

From Opium to Cotton

The start of the 18th century saw a gradual reversal in the new colony's fortunes. Drainage work slowly improved the health of its inhabitants. Blockaded by the Moghuls and with its port silting up, Surat was also on the wane and its trade haemorrhaging to Bombay. Then, in 1739, the Portuguese threat was dispelled when the Marathas took Bassein. It would be another 60 years before French designs on the sub-continent were decisively foiled, with their defeat alongside Tipu Sultan of Mysore in the Battle of Seringapatnam, but the Napoleonic wars did prompt the EIC to upgrade the fort and walls around what had by now become a thriving, densely populated town.

Two events at the end of the century were to prove central to Bombay's meteoric expansion, which in under 100 years would see it grow to become the largest city in the East after

Bombay Harbour, around 1730

Tokyo. The first was a famine in China. With Chinese cotton fields taken out of production to grow grain, prices of Indian cotton rocketed. This enabled traders in Bombay to procure much cheaper tea, for which demand had surged since duties on it had been cut in England. Over time, these two commodities started to supplant opium as the port's principal stock in trade. Mercantile activity in Bombay received another boost

City sweetmeat trader, c.1830

in 1833, when the EIC's monopoly was finally repealed, encouraging international traders – notably Sephardic Jews from Baghdad – to join the Banias and Parsi merchants, who were by that time making big money in the colony.

British Women Arrive

An influx of a less overtly commercial nature started to make its mark on Bombay through the 1830s and 1840s. The advent of steamers and a new, faster 'overland' route to India via Cairo and Suez (which cut journey times from seven to three months) saw significant numbers of British women coming to India for the first time. The docking of the annual 'fishing fleet', as the ships of unmarried damsels hoping to find husbands here was dubbed, was eagerly awaited.

Life in Bombay was to be radically transformed by the arrival of the 'Memsahib'. For a start, liaisons with native women – hitherto tolerated, and enjoyed by men of all ranks, albeit discreetly – became frowned upon. In common with Europe, colonial society as a whole also grew steadily more snobbish and status-conscious. This despite the manifest British dependency on their Parsi middlemen, who had by now become the colony's bankers, financiers, charitable benefactors, shipwrights and main property owners.

Cotton Mania and Independence

Bombay stood calmly by as the rest of British India reeled after the 1857 Bengal Uprising. Its merchants were far too preoccupied with a new cotton boom to consider 'mutiny'. The American Civil War had blocked exports of cotton from the southern Confederacy states, sending prices of Indian cotton sky high once again. Many fortunes were made – but as many lost when the inevitable crash came with the end of the war in 1864. Bombay, however, continued to boom.

The inauguration of the Great Indian Peninsula Railway in 1863, which connected the city with its cotton suppliers on the Deccan, coupled with the opening of the Suez Canal six years later, saw the port soon eclipse Calcutta as Britain's *Urbis Prima* in India. The 1860s and 1870s are when the Bombay as it now stands largely took shape: when Governor Bartle Frere pulled down the old fort's walls to make room for the giant Gothic-Revival piles that still dominate the downtown districts; when the docks were expanded and large areas of land reclaimed to join the seven islands together; and when the northern suburbs were engulfed by an appalling industrial sprawl of mills and slums. Living conditions in the thick of this metropolis were, by all accounts, squalid, and in 1891 300 people were dying each week in an outbreak of bubonic plague that sent half the population fleeing to the countryside.

The visit of King George V and Queen Mary to Bombay in 1911, commemorated by the Gateway of India, is general-

The visit of George V and Queen Mary, 1911

ly regarded as the high watermark of Raj power in Bombay. But by then cracks in the façade of British rule were starting to show. Rioting sparked off by Mohandas K. (Mahatma) Gandhi's appeal for a boycott of the celebrations marking the arrival of the Prince of Wales (later King Edward VII) in 1921 killed 58. Gandhi also chose Bombay as the launch pad for his 'Quit India' campaign in 1942, which led to the bungled departure of the British five years later.

Post-Independence

Since Independence, Bombay – or Mumbai as it was renamed in 1996 – has continued to grow at exponential rates, spreading northwards over newly reclaimed land. Poor migrants from the countryside still pour in by their tens of thousands each year in search of better lives in the city. But lack of adequate housing and jobs forces many into ever-swelling slums and pavement shanties.

Resentment at this massive influx, in fact at the very cosmopolitanism that has always been the defining feature of the city, was a major factor behind the rise of the right-wing, pro-Hindu, pro-Maharashtran party, the Shiv Sena. Led by a former cartoonist and self-confessed admirer of Hitler, Bal Thackery, the Sena (literally 'Shiva's Army') and its militaristic cadres exploited disaffection among working-class Marathis to dominate the city's politics throughout the 1980s. Its leaders orchestrated the appalling riots of December 1992–January 1993, which ripped through the heart of the city in the wake of the destruction by Hindu fundamentalists of the Babri Masjid mosque in Ayodhya, northern India. Thousands died in massacres, the majority of them Muslims, and when a series of devastating explosions paralysed the city a few months later, it was widely interpreted as retaliation by Muslim gangsters.

Organised crime and communal politics are still to the fore in the Maharashtran capital, which the Shiv Sena-dominated muncipality renamed Mumbai in 1995 as part of a sweeping attempt to 're-Hinduise' the city. Other colonial-era names fell foul of the rebranding exercise – including Victoria Terminus and Sahar international airport.

The youth of today

In spite of its problems, the city continues to spearhead South Asia's awesome economic growth. Representative of the rest of India it might not be, but as the engine room of Indian finance and trade, Mumbai is still embracing new technologies and ways of making money to shape the country's future.

Historical Landmarks

2nd century AD The first cave-shrines and monasteries are excavated on the hills at Kanheri.

6th century Kalchuri dynasty carves a Hindu temple at Elephanta Island, then part of major trading city, Gheranpuri.

1662 Charles II receives Bombay in Catherine of Braganza's dowry.

1760s and 1770s The fort's defences are upgraded in response to the threat from the French. Famine in China pushes up the price of cotton.

1803 Fire devastates the fort; 471 houses are destroyed.

1830s The end of pirate attacks and the advent of steamers brings white 'memsahibs' to Bombay in large numbers for the first time.

1853 Inauguration of the Great Indian Peninsula Railway.

1857 'Cotton Mania' due to American Civil War. Share prices soar.

1864 Telegraph cable laid via Persian Gulf. Its first message announces the end of the American Civil War, provoking a nose dive in cotton prices and a stock market crash.

1869 Suez Canal opens. Bombay becomes British India's main port. A massive building boom ensues.

1921 Riots greet the Prince of Wales's arrival in city, following Mahatma Gandhi's plea to boycott celebrations; 58 die.

1947 The end of British rule is marked with the departure of the last troops on Indian soil from Bombay's Gateway of India.

1992–3 Appalling communal riots follow the destruction of the Babri Masjid mosque in Ayodhya; at least 1,400 die and 150,000 flee the city – most of them Muslims. Three months later, Muslim gangsters set off 10 bombs in the heart of Bombay, as a reprisal for the earlier pogroms, killing 317.

1996 Nationalist party, Shiv Sena, renames Bombay 'Mumbai'.

25 August 2003 Two bombs explode in the city, one of them next to the Gateway of India; 107 die.

26 July 2005 The highest rainfall – 942mm (37.1in) – recorded in a city in a 24-hour period falls on Mumbai. Landslides and flooding cause the deaths of more than 100 people and strand 150,000.

WHERE TO GO

Mumbai grew more rapidly than any of India's other great metropolitan cities, and what few monuments there were before the arrival of the Portuguese and British tended, with some notable exceptions, to get swept aside in the name of progress. As a consequence, this isn't a destination full of unmissable sights. Plenty of wonderful monuments do survive from its colonial heyday, but in many ways travelling between them is where the real interest lies. Immerse yourself in Mumbai's teeming street life – rubbing shoulders with commuters at rush hour, or jostling with porters in the stations and bazaars – and you'll get a vivid sense of what makes the Maharashtran capital such an extraordinary place to live and work.

> **Mumbai's highlights are featured on the local tourist corporation MTDC's popular half-day sightseeing tours. For more on these, *see page 116.***

Mumbai's historic patina makes the most impact in the southern part of the peninsula, where the giant buildings of the late-19th century cotton boom form a grandiose backdrop. This account begins where all tours of the city should start, at the majestic Gateway of India in Colaba, and from there progresses north through the Fort district, the throbbing business heart of Mumbai, to the breezier climes of Back Bay, Chowpatty Beach and Malabar Hill in the west, where a few fascinating vestiges of pre-colonial times still lurk among the ritzy skyscrapers. Further north, the labyrinthine bazaars of central Mumbai extend into the

Mumbai marathon runners make their way along Marine Drive

poorer, tightly packed core of the metropolis, where you could wander for weeks without passing the same street corner twice.

For a respite from the traffic fumes and crowds, these days Mumbaikars – at least those who can afford it – head north to the affluent suburbs of Bandra and Juhu, where some of the city's smartest shops, restaurants and hotels line up within easy reach of the seafront. But you can escape the urban sprawl completely by catching a boat out to Elephanta Island, in Mumbai harbour. There, at the top of a wooded hill, a Hindu cave temple shelters some of India's finest ancient sculpture, hollowed out from the rock in the 6th century AD.

On the waterfront

Still older caves are hidden in the green hills floating above Mumbai's northern fringes in the Sanjay Gandhi National Park – another popular daytrip.

Visits to these historic sites inspire many to tackle longer excursions into Maharashtra proper. To the southeast, the cave complexes at Karla and Bhaja can be reached in a day's round trip, but you'd be better off combining them with a visit to the little hill station of Matheran, connected to the plains 750m (2,460ft) below via a tiny narrow-gauge train. These caves, however, are mere small fry compared with the much larger and stylistically evolved excavations that lie a day's journey away to the northeast.

Deep in the arid hills of the Deccan Plateau, UNESCO-listed Ellora and Ajanta are Maharashtra's main visitor attractions and, quite simply, are among the world's greatest repositories of ancient art and culture.

COLABA

Colaba, at the south end of the peninsula, has since Victorian times been most visitors' first landfall in Mumbai, and remains its chief tourist hub. As the site of the city's most famous landmark, the Gateway of India, and glamorous hotel, the Taj Mahal Palace and Tower, the district attracts working-class daytrippers and the wealthy city set in equal numbers. A rolling jamboree of bus parties, balloon hawkers, itinerant photographers and snack *wallahs* revolves around the square at its heart, open to the sea breezes on one side.

But this is only a small part of the picture. Head south down Colaba's main thoroughfare (Shahid Bhagat Singh Marg, or 'Colaba Causeway' as it used to be known) and soon the busy streets and wood-fronted colonial tenements start to give way to a leafy cantonment, eventually petering out at a sea wall where a solitary lighthouse crowns the city's most southerly point.

Less than 150 years ago, this whole area lay entirely under water. Only at the end of the 19th century was reclamation work completed and Colaba's various islets fused into a single mass. Thereafter, the district (whose name derives from the Koli fishing caste who inhabited it long before the arrival of the Europeans) became Bombay's principal landing stage. P&O steamers arriving from London would tie up alongside its quay, **Apollo Bunder**, and their passengers, after several weeks at sea, would alight here for their first taste of India.

The only boats rolling in the swell beneath the Gateway of India these days tend to be excursion launches waiting to ferry trippers out to Elephanta Island. But the slightly seedy edge to the port that Colaba once was still hangs over some of its back streets, where prostitutes ply their trade from doorways and pavement sleepers huddle over opium pipes in dark corners. Not that this deters the city's affluent classes from coming here in the least, for at weekends the same back streets will be jammed with luxury cars while their owners patronise the many trendy restaurants, bars and clubs standing in the shadow of the Taj.

For many foreign visitors, Colaba *is* Mumbai. Lined with street markets, air-conditioned souvenir emporia, Western-style cafés, hip clothes shops, banks and travel agents, it holds just about every facility a tourist could want, while the city's finest museum and handful of art galleries lie only a short walk to the north.

The Gateway of India

The triple-arched **Gateway of India** is Colaba's focal point and Mumbai's most instantly recognisable monument. Inscribed in strident Times-Roman letters across its parapet is a reminder that the triumphal arch was erected in 1924 to commemorate the visit to the city of King George V and Queen Mary 13 years earlier. Its architect, George Wittet, incorporated into his design many Indian elements, such as pierced-stone *jali* screens and Gujarati brackets. But in spirit, the structure was, and still remains, essentially imperial

The aboriginal Koli fishing caste that first inhabited Bombay harbour still lives in shanty settlements around Colaba and Nariman Point, their shacks and boats standing in stark contrast to the skyscrapers looming on all sides.

The triple-arched Gateway of India

– no other building erected in British India possesses such grandiloquence, and in its day the Gateway became the defining symbol of the Raj.

It is all the more ironic, therefore, that the arch will also forever be associated with the British Empire's final days. In August 1947, amid much pomp, the remaining foreign troops on Indian soil slow-marched beneath it to board the steamer that would take them home, as the Union Jack was lowered for the last time.

Modern Mumbaikars and their compatriots are no less proud of the Gateway than the British were. Since Independence, Indians have flocked here to pay homage to the edifice whose image has become famous as the backdrop to innumerable Bollywood song and dance numbers. Sadly, the same iconic status also made the Gateway a terrorist target: on 25 August, 2003, Muslim extremists exploded a car bomb in the piazza near it, killing 107 people.

Taj Mahal Palace and Tower

The Taj Mahal Hotel

Facing the Gateway of India from the opposite side of Apollo Bunder is colonial Bombay's other great showpiece, the **Taj Mahal Hotel** (or the Taj Mahal Palace and Tower, as it's officially called these days). Despite being, in the words of Jan Morris, 'the quintessence of Imperial amplitude', the building was in fact commissioned by a Parsi called Jamesetji Nusserwanji Tata. Legend has it that the enterprising J.N.T. conceived the idea as a snub to the owners of what was then the city's premier hotel, the 'whites only' Watson's, which once refused him entry on the grounds of race.

Constructed in 1903, the Taj was an eloquent repost. In spite or because of the fact that it opened its doors to anyone wealthy enough to afford its prices, the hotel was immediately embraced by Bombay's wealthy elite and remains *the* place to be seen (Watson's, on the other hand, closed years ago).

Its original entrance was to the rear – not, as is often supposed, because of an architect's error, but in order to maximise the number of rooms which could have uninterrupted sea views. Today, the main lobby has been moved to the northern corner, close to the Gateway of India. Non-residents are welcome inside to sample the delights of the hotel's gourmet restaurants, pastry shops and to browse the luxury boutiques in the air-conditioned shopping arcades. But the real character of the place lies inside its old wing, where wood-balustraded corridors are stacked seven floors high, like a luxury Edwardian prison wing.

For the best views of the hotel's exterior you should jump on one of the launches bound for Elephanta Island *(see page 66)*. From the sea, the Taj – with a grey and white façade, red domes, arches, Swiss gables and elaborate corner towers – exudes grandeur. The rather less sightly skyscraper standing next to it is the modern wing of the hotel, likened by the journalist James Cameron to 'an aristocratic lady in a sports car'.

Sassoon Docks and Afghan Church

Two sights warrant a detour to the south end of Colaba. The first of them, **Sassoon Docks**, is where the city's busy trawler fleet lands its catch each morning. If you can cope with the overpowering stench, wander around the quays to watch the fish being flung into crates full of ice balancing on the heads

Early morning at Sassoon Docks

Sassoon Docks' young sailors

of waiting porters, who carry them at top speed to the adjacent auction halls for sale. Literally hundreds of boats tie up here during the day, their massed flags, masts and rigs forming one of Mumbai's more arresting spectacles. This is also where you are bound to catch a glimpse of the city's signature dish, 'Bombay duck', being dried in the salty breezes *(see page 45)*.

In the far south of the district, past the naval base and military cantonment, stands another evocative colonial monument. Though nowadays it's dwarfed by the skyscrapers rising from nearby Nariman Point, the slender, tapering steeple of the **Afghan Church of Saint John the Baptist** once dominated Bombay's skyline. It was built as a memorial to the thousands of British soldiers who died in the campaigns of Sind and Afghanistan between 1835 and 1843. Memorial plaques in white, red, ochre and grey-blue marble line the walls of the chancels, listing officers killed in action. The names of the other ranks who fell alongside them were going to be inscribed on vellum scrolls, but the project ran out of money. You can, however, admire the colours of some of the regiments involved in the wars, among them the East India Company's Bombay Army, which was annihilated in the infamous expedition to Kabul in 1842.

KALA GHODA

Until Independence a black equestrian statue of Edward VII presided over the square just north of Colaba, where MG Road converges on Subhash Chowk. This was long ago pulled down, but its nickname in Marathi, '*Kala Ghoda*' (Black Statue), has survived to denote the district which, in recent years, has rebranded itself as a centre for culture and the arts. No visit to Mumbai would be complete without a look around its grand centrepiece, the Chhatrapati Shivaji (formerly Prince of Wales) Museum, which holds a collection of antiquities unrivalled outside Delhi; while on the opposite side of the road, a pair of galleries showcases the work of contemporary artists.

The Museum and Galleries

The former **Prince of Wales Museum of Western India**, or **Chhatrapati Shivaji Maharaj Vastu Sangrahalaya** (open Tues–Sun 10.15am–6pm; admission fee), to give it its more politically correct Marathi name, occupies a building which typifies the more whimsical tendencies of late-Raj architecture. Dreamed up by George Wittet (of Gateway of India fame), its design blends elements of medieval Gujarat and Bijapur with municipal London and Manchester – to memorable effect. This so-called Indo-Saracenic style has had its detractors (not least the art critic and author of *The Road to Oxiana*, Robert Byron, who famously dubbed Victorian Bombay as 'an architectural sodom'). But the impact of the museum's striped basalt bricks, minarets, Islamic arches and

On Sundays throughout December and January, the intersection outside the museum complex is cleared of cars and given over to the lively Kala Ghoda Fair, in which artists and crafts people from across the city sell their work.

bulbous, mock-Moghul dome today comes across as quirky rather than pompous.

Inside, the museum's collection is displayed amid conditions that can have altered little since the building's opening. The **Key Gallery** on the ground floor assembles some of the highlights, notably the famous 5th-century Buddhist figures unearthed by Henry Cousens at Mirpur Khas in 1909. These include an exquisite standing male holding a lotus flower – one of India's finest archaeological treasures. Also on the ground floor, the **Sculpture Gallery** mostly holds fragments of Hindu temple carvings, among them a resplendent Brahma seated on a lotus from Aihole (in neighbouring Karnataka state). But the most ancient exhibits here are Buddhist: 4th- and 5th-century terracotta heads bearing distinct traces of Greek influence.

Upstairs, a world-renowned collection of Indian **miniature painting** features pages from the libraries of no less than the Moghul emperors themselves, while in the **Meherbhai Khandalawala Gallery** down the corridor you can admire ornate Gujarati wood carvings, more beautiful Gandharan figures and some superb Chola bronzes from the Tamil south.

Much of the upper levels of the museum are given over to missable cases of glass and ceramic objects from China, and European oil paintings (including a minor Titian and a Constable). But hidden away in a side gallery is a gruesome display of medieval Indian weaponry featuring Emperor Akbar's own jade dagger and body armour, the latter bearing an inscription in Persian that was only recently translated to reveal the identity of its illustrious owner.

The best place to grab a sandwich and cold drink between trips to the museum is the Café Samovar, accessed via the Jehangir Art Gallery. For a review, *see page 137.*

Moghul miniature in the Prince of Wales Museum

Adjacent to the Chhatrapati Shivaji Museum stands the **Jehangir Art Gallery** (open daily 11am–7pm; free), where exhibitions of contemporary art are laid on throughout the year. Its small terrace café, the Samovar *(see page 137)*, is a favourite haunt of the city's intelligentsia and art collectors, and makes an ideal place to recover from the travails of sightseeing. Mumbai's other notable art venue is the **National Gallery of Modern Art**, or NGMO (open Tues–Sun 10am–5pm; admission fee), a short walk down MG Road from the museum. Occupying a former concert hall, it traces the evolution of contemporary Indian art across five decades, culminating in a floor of lively installations.

Oval Maidan and Bombay University

Some of Victorian Bombay's most imposing buildings line the western flanks of Kala Ghoda. Great brooding piles sprouting vast arcaded verandahs and spiky towers, they date from the boom of the 1860s and 1870s when this was the western edge of the city, or Esplanade. Bombay's governor, Sir Bartle Frere, had decided to open up the expanding Fort area to fresh sea air by dismantling the old ramparts, and recruited some of the era's most promising architects to draw up plans for a spectacular new seafront. Rising dramatically from the foreshore, the buildings must have presented an awesome spectacle to those arriving in Bombay by ship; this was said at the time to be the grandest sight in the entire British Empire. But the reclamation of Back Bay in the 1920s left the row high and dry, and it now overlooks the parched fields of **Oval Maidan**, the remnants of the old 'field of fire'

Bombay University

that extended from the fort's walls. Today, the space functions as a park where cricketers in proper whites play in the blazing afternoon heat.

Dominating the eastern side of the *maidan* is the old Bombay **Secretariat**. 'A massive pile whose main features have been brought from Venice but all the beauty has vanished in the transhipment' was how civil servant G.W. Forrest described it in 1903.

To more charitable modern eyes, the enormous building (which now houses the City Civil and Sessions Court) possesses a certain nobility, with gigantic pitched roofs and balconies shaded by enormous rattan blinds.

Next door, **Bombay University** comprises some of the most admired and abused buildings in the city. The extravagantly Gothic Revival campus was designed by Sir Gilbert Scott, then at the peak of his career, having completed work on those other Gothic showpieces, the Albert Memorial and St Pancras Station in London. Scott's challenge was to come up with plans for a university which, unlike the ones in Britain it would be

Venerable statue at the university

modelled on, was to be resolutely secular (its students being mostly Hindus and Muslims). The result, though devoid of religious imagery, still smacks of Christian Oxbridge, only with turbaned kings and queens in exotic Oriental garb where you might expect to see saints or bearded benefactors.

A Christian-Gothic spirit also pervades the high-roofed **Convocation Hall**, whose wonderful stained-glass window features the signs of the zodiac. Reached by an elaborately decorated spiral staircase, the adjacent **library** is, as Jan Morris put it 'Oxbridge absolute', down to the wood panelling, glass bookcases and vaulted reading room.

Rising above it, the **Rajabhai Clock Tower** is said to have taken its cue from Giotto's campanile in Florence, but with more statues personifying the castes and communities of western India added to the exterior walls. Prior to the construction of the stock exchange, it used to be the tallest building in Bombay, and would regale the city's inhabitants with chiming renditions of *Rule Britannia* and *God Save the King*, on the hour.

FORT

Having taken possession of the seven Bombay islands from the Portuguese in 1668, the British East India Company set about strengthening their new territory with a mighty stone fort. Construction work on the project spanned 50 years. When it was finished, a vast area on the largest island's eastern seaboard was encircled in sloping ramparts, moats and

Dabawallas

Indians often assert that there's no better food than proper home cooking, and in Mumbai the maxim fuels its own mini industry, set up to transfer freshly prepared lunches from 16,000 housewives' kitchens in the suburbs to their husbands' offices in the centre. The cogs in this complex machine are members of the grandly titled **Nutun Mumbai Tiffin Box Suppliers Charity Trust**, an army of cotton-clad porters affectionately known by Mumbaikars as *dabawallas*.

Each morning, over a thousand of them can be seen scurrying over railway platforms, shifting headtrays, shoulder poles and bicycles loaded with little round, three-tiered tins. These tiffin boxes, containing portions of curry, *dal*, rice and neatly folded *chapattis*, will have been collected from individual homes across suburban Mumbai and taken to the nearest railway stations. Handed through chains of different *dabawallas*, they eventually emerge at Churchgate Station in the city centre, where they are piled on to handcarts and pushed, amid much waving and shouting, through the streets of the commercial district to their final destinations.

The service, operated by men from a single village near Pune, is extraordinarily cheap and efficient. Thanks to a time-honoured colour code painted on the boxes' lids, their mostly illiterate carriers lose only an estimated one in six million, putting the *dabawallas* on a par with the world's slickest blue-chip companies in efficiency terms.

clear field of fire. Three for-
tified gateways gave access
to the rapidly expanding
town inside, divided be-
tween the European quarters
in the south and native ones
in the north.

By the mid-19th century,
with British rule finally
unassailable in India, the
fort had become largely re-
dundant and its boundaries
confined those of the bur-
geoning city. Sir Bartle
Frere, therefore, gave orders
for the ramparts to be pulled
down. Today, barely a frag-

**A Mumbai *dabawalla* delivers
his tiffin boxes**

ment of the old walls remains, but their ghostly presence
continues to be felt. Still known as 'Fort', the area they once
enclosed has retained more historic character than any other
part of the city. Lined by magnificent polychromatic buildings, its labyrinthine grid plan harbours rows of mildewing
department stores and banks, Parsi fire temples, stationery
suppliers, printers, publishers, newspaper offices and hole-
in-the-wall cafés. This is an especially atmospheric place to
wander at lunchtime or just at the end of the working day,
when office-*wallahs* in their thousands stream through the
streets, pausing for a plate of *pao bhaji* or a paper cone of
gram from the braziers smoking on the pavements.

Horniman Circle and the Town Hall

The main east–west artery through Fort is straddled by a perfectly round public park, laid out in the 1860s on the last remaining patch of Bombay Green (a parade ground where

cotton was also bailed and dispatched in the 18th century). Originally called Elphinstone Circle, after Lord Mountstuart Elphinstone (one of Bombay's more influential 19th-century governors), it was renamed **Horniman Circle** after Independence, in honour of a former newspaper editor and freedom fighter. The garden's typically British wrought-iron gates and fences enclose a haven of greenery where white collar workers bring their tiffin boxes and newspapers during lunch hours. Forming the heart of the city's first planned financial district, the buildings surrounding it are exceptionally grand, though in recent times seem to have fallen out of fashion. Families of street dwellers have set up home in their ground-floor arcades, watched by the rows of grim-faced keystone heads crowning the arches above.

Overlooking the western end of Horniman Circle, separated from the rest of Fort by the busy Shahid Bhagat Singh Marg,

The Horniman Circle public park

stands the old **Town Hall**. Erected in 1833, the building was conceived by its designer, one Colonel Thomas Cooper of the Bombay Engineers, in high neo-Classical style, complete with fluted Doric columns and broad,

> It was at the top of the Town Hall's imposing flight of steps that Queen Victoria herself read the historic decree dissolving the East India Company in 1858.

low pediment. The design was acclaimed in its day as a masterpiece, and even Aldous Huxley, who loathed everything else he was shown in Bombay, confessed himself an admirer. Cooper's *piece de résistance*, however, was the interior. Once beyond the monumental flight of 30 steps fronting the building, you enter a central hall illuminated by beams of light from high louvred windows. A pair of elegant spiral staircases sweep up its sides, past white marble statues of various imperial grandees; the effect is oddly theatrical.

While the main parts of the building hosted government and cultural functions, the north wing of the Town Hall was set aside for the **Royal Asiatic Society Library**, whose collection now forms part of the **State Central Library** (open Mon–Sat 10am–7pm). Along with copies of every book printed in India, the archives include more than 10,000 rare antique manuscripts, among them a copy of Dante's *Divine Comedy* rumoured to be worth US$3 million – Mussolini tried to buy it once but was turned down. The whole place is locked in a delicious Raj-era time warp, its teak shelves stuffed with leather-bound volumes, many of them mouldering away in the humid half-light.

St Thomas's Cathedral

The oldest surviving building in Mumbai is thought to be **St Thomas's Cathedral**, on the opposite side of Horniman Circle to the Town Hall. A hotchpotch of Classical and

Stained glass in St Thomas's

Gothic styles, it started out life in the 1670s as a roof-less garrison church, and might have stayed that way had it not been for the cajoling of an energetic young chaplain, Richard Cobbe. He arrived in Bombay in 1714 to find the colony's main place of worship with 'trees growing out of the stonework'. He quickly set about raising funds to finish the job and on Christmas Day 1718, a new church, complete with traditional Indian cow-dung floor, oyster shell windows, canon-proof roof and box pews for 'inferior women', was duly opened for worship.

With the arrival in the mid-19th century of a new breed of evangelical Christians, the church acquired an extension, a new steeple and, in 1833, cathedral status. Smothered in cream paint, St Thomas's today strikes an incongruous note against the bare stone facades of the old financial hub next to it, but deserves a visit. Fixed to the walls inside it are dozens of memorial plaques to East India Company and government officials who suffered a variety of unpleasant ends in the service of the British Empire, from death in battle to tropical diseases. One, Lieutenant Henry Robertson Bower of the Royal Indian Marines 'lost his life returning from the South Pole with Scott'.

Veer Nariman Road runs west from the old cathedral through the congested heart of Fort to one of modern Mumbai's busiest intersections, **Hutatma Chowk**, or Martyrs' Square, where a memorial to Maharashtran freedom fighters stands alongside a rather more whimsical fountain, long dried up. It was originally commissioned in 1869 as a memorial to Sir Bartle Frere, one of Bombay's more committed civic reformers, but this fact was from the outset eclipsed by the scantily clad figure of the Roman goddess Flora that stood as its centrepiece, and Bombayites have always referred to it as simply '**Flora Fountain**'. Carved from Portland stone (which the local municipality annually spoils with a coat of white paint), the memorial stands slap in the centre of a large square which, when it isn't clogged with parked cars and street stalls, hosts noisy political rallies.

The 'Flora Fountain' in Martyr's Square

Chhatrapati Shivaji Terminus (Victoria Terminus) ◄

On 16 April, 1853, accompanied by brass bands and considerable pomp, the first railway line in India was inaugurated. It ran only 34km (21 miles), from a temporary wooden hut on Bori Bunder quay just north of Bombay Fort, to the island of Thane. But this was the just the beginning of a project that would, by the end of the century, have changed the course of history for millions: the Great Indian Peninsula Railway.

Three decades on, the shack marking the start of the line was replaced by a building its creators intended not merely as a station, but a symbol of all the British Empire had thus far achieved, of its pride, power and seemingly boundless

Chhatrapati Shivaji (formerly Victoria) Terminus

potential. The world had never seen the likes of **Victoria Terminus**, or 'VT', as the behemoth was christened on Jubilee Day 1887 – and it would never do so again. Conceived on a vast scale, greater even than that other Victorian Gothic monster, St Pancras, it amalgamated all the stylistic eccentricities of the day: ornate domes, minarets, pinnacles and towers, loggias, buttresses, fancy arched windows and a staggering wealth of sculptural detail. Lady Dufferin, the Vicereine, declared it 'perfectly magnificent' and the public, by and large, agreed (although some found the whole thing decidedly over the top for a mere railway station).

Renamed **Chhatrapati Shivaji Terminus** (CST) in 1996, VT today remains one of the country's landmark buildings, much loved and admired in spite of its imperial associations. Viewed from the opposite side of Dadabhai Naoroji Road (outside McDonald's), the general plan comes into relief. High on the central dome, a statue of 'Progress' with her arm raised prophetically sails above three huge gables, each crowned by other allegorical figures representing 'Engineering', 'Commerce' and 'Agriculture' respectively. Below them, the main west entrance to what now serves as the headquarters of the Central Railway is flanked by a 'British' lion and 'Indian' recumbent tiger. Sculpted portraits of Queen Victoria, the Viceroy, the chief railway engineer and other imperial worthies look impassively down, as they have been since the traffic swirling around below them was horse-drawn.

It's well worth venturing inside to see the station's resplendent interior decor. The Director of the Bombay Arts School, Lockwood Kipling (Rudyard's father) recruited his top students for the job of embellishing VT, and no expense was spared. The combined effect of the elaborate stonework (in coloured marble and polished Aberdeen granite), of the richly carved wood, of the panels and friezes of birds, animals and plants, and of the stained glass and painted ceilings, is sumptuous.

The building's chief architect, F.W. Stevens, lived just long enough to see his grand design completed, and to receive the praise it deserved. Regardless of whether or not his efforts are appreciated by the tens of thousands of travellers who pour

---

Bombay Duck

The very mention of it may conjure up visions of fowl curry, but 'Bombay duck' is in fact a fish – to be precise, the 'marine lizard fish', *Harpalon nehereus* ('*bummalo*' in Maharathi). Its English name is thought to derive from the Hindustani for mail train, *dak*. The fish's unpleasant odour apparently reminded Bombayites of the rank smell of the Calcutta–Bombay *dak* when it pulled in to Victoria Terminus after three days and nights on the rails, its wooden carriages covered in stinking mould from the monsoon rains.

through his station each day, the splendour creates a wonderful counterpoint to the river of life you plunge into on the main concourse: passengers from across India weave through crowds of ticket collectors, red-shirted porters, *dabawallas*, mendicant *sadhus*, *chai* sellers, coolies pushing handcarts piled with fish baskets, and row upon row of sleeping bodies.

The General Post Office

Another charismatic vestige of the Raj stands a short walk east from VT down Walchand Hirachand Marg (Fort St). Completed in 1911, the **General Post Office** (GPO) is generally considered as one of the more successful examples of the much-derided Indo-Saracenic school of architecture, which sought to integrate Indian motifs into civic design. Here, the Golgumbaz tomb in Bijapur clearly provided much inspiration, not least for the huge dome that crowns the building. Directly beneath it, in the main hall, ranks of clerks doze behind the original circular Victorian counter, while pigeons flit perilously between the paddle fans high overhead. You can browse first-day covers at the Philatelic Bureau down the corridor, or just wander aimlessly around soaking up visions of the old-fashioned Indian bureaucracy that still holds sway here.

> In the little square opposite the GPO, a curious fenced enclosure is the 18th-century Kothari Kaboota Khanna, or pigeon feeding station, where local Jains donate grain for the city's wild birds. You can buy the seeds for a couple of rupees from a hole-in-the-wall stall nearby.

Indian parcels have to be stitched in white cotton and sealed with wax before posting, and on the pavement opposite the GPO, rows of letter writers and parcel-*wallahs* sit cross-legged patiently waiting for trade.

MARINE DRIVE

Marine Drive, Mumbai's own Sunset Boulevard, sweeps in a dramatic arc from the skyscrapers of Nariman Point to the foot of Malabar Hill in the north. Built on land reclaimed from Back Bay less than a century ago, it provides the city's pedestrians with welcome access to the sea, and its motorised traffic with a fast, eight-lane bypass. The wide promenade running along the sea wall affords fine views of the urban skyline and is a popular place for a sunset stroll. For the best panorama, however, you'll have to shell out on a meal or room at the Oberoi *(see page 132)*, whose upper floors survey the 3-km (2-mile) chain of lights that give Marine Drive the nickname Queen's Necklace.

Beyond a rank of peeling Art Deco apartment blocks, there's little of note along the route until you reach the old

Marine Drive

Windmill seller, Chowpatty Beach

gymkhanas midway up. With cricket greens and pavilions, these typically British 'clubs' were established by separate communities – Catholics, Muslims, Hindus and Parsis – as replicas of their 'Europeans Only' counterparts elsewhere in the city, several of which refused membership to Indians until World War II.

Chowpatty Beach

Chowpatty Beach, at the north end of Marine Drive, occupies a place close to the hearts of most Mumbaikars. It is where many of them were brought as children to play on rusty Ferris wheels, munch *bhel puri* and *kulfi*, and snigger at the courting couples, and where they bring their own kids today. Chowpatty is also a popular venue for political rallies (it hosted some epoch-making demos during the freedom struggle) and occasionally music concerts and movies. A clean-up campaign has weeded out some of the more disreputable elements that formerly added colour to beach life, notably the card tricksters, ear cleaners, *bhang* sellers and busking eunuchs *(hijras)*, who have shifted north to work Juhu Beach *(see page 62)*, but it remains a fun place to while away an hour or two, especially around sunset and on Sunday afternoons.

However, Chowpatty's really big day is in August or September, when hundreds of thousands of Hindus gather here to immerse their outsized effigies of the elephant-headed god, Ganpati, in the sea during the Ganesh Chaturthi festival *(see page 95)*. Visitors who are unaccustomed to mass Indian religious gatherings are best advised, should they be here at that time, to get no closer to the frenzied proceedings than an adjacent rooftop.

Mani Bhavan

Since his unsuccessful attempt to pursue a career as a barrister in 1891, Mohandas K. (Mahatma) Gandhi was a frequent visitor to Bombay. Throughout his Satyagraha (literally 'grasping of truth') campaign, he spent long spells in the city organising strikes *(hartals)* among the textile workers, addressing rallies and negotiating with British officials. On one occasion, his plea to the masses to boycott the arrival of the Prince of Wales (later King Edward VII) in 1921 resulted in terrible riots – those Indians (mainly Parsis) who insisted on taking part in the reception were, much to Gandhi's dismay, attacked by mobs and 58 died. The famous 'Quit India' movement that proved the death blow for British rule was also launched here in 1942.

Belonging to a diamond merchant, **Mani Bhavan**, the house where he stayed, in a leafy suburb not far from Chowpatty, has been turned into a museum (open daily 9.30am–6pm; admission fee) housing a modest collection of photographs and what few possessions the Mahatma had. These include the spinning wheel he allegedly learned to spin on, his string bed *(charpoi)*, library and some personal letters, among them one written to Hitler in the 1930s asking him to desist from aggression in Europe.

Mani Bhavan is at 19 Laburnum Road, close to August Kranti (also known as Gowalia Tank) Maidan, 10 minutes' walk inland from Chowpatty seaface along P. Ramabai Marg (Harvey Road).

MALABAR HILL

The steep sided promontory enfolding Chowpatty Beach at the northern end of Back Bay is known as **Malabar Hill** after the Malabari pirates who are supposed to have had a hideout here in pre-colonial times. It has long been Mumbai's most desirable neighbourhood, since the first British governors and merchants chose it as a site for their mansions, attracted by its salubrious breezes, leafy woodland and panoramic views. These, and most of the trees, have been supplanted by high-rise apartment blocks belonging to the city's mega-rich. But hidden among the skyscrapers are a few dilapidated remains of Mumbai's pre-colonial past that deserve a detour.

The Banganga Tank and Walukeshwar Temple

Prior to the arrival of the Europeans, the islands of Bombay were scattered with Hindu temples and sacred bathing

---

The Towers of Silence

The Zoroastrians or Parsis are from Persia. They arrived on the Indian coast in around AD650, and in the 18th century were among the first communities to respond to British calls to populate the new colony of Bombay. The more devout descendents of these first immigrants, though dwindling in numbers, still adhere to ancient tenets forbidding burial or cremation, which are believed to defile the sacred elements of earth and fire. Instead, Parsis dispose of their dead by leaving the corpses for vultures to feast on in special structures called Towers of Silence, or *dokhmas*, seven of which still stand in one of the last surviving patches of woodland on Malabar Hill. Screened from prying eyes by high walls, the mortuary ground is off-limits to all but the caste of Zoroastrian pall bearers responsible for preparing the bodies for the birds, which you can see perched on the neighbourhood trees.

tanks, or *tirthas*. Only one survives, at the end of the Malabar promontory. Believed to have been created by an arrow fired from the god Rama's bow, on his epic journey to rescue Sita from the evil demon Ravana in Lanka, the **Banganga Tank** is all the more extraordinary for having endured in the midst of some of the world's most expensive real estate. Yet endure it has, seemingly unchanged for hundreds, or possibly thousands, of years. Pilgrims still bathe from its stepped sides, changing and resting in the ramshackle hostels surrounding it before making the auspicious clock-

Banganga, the city's last surviving sacred bathing tank

wise walk around the rectangular pool and sacred wooden pole (or *stambha*) in its centre.

Among the dozen or so shrines clustered on Banganga's western bank, the **Walukeshwar Temple** is the most important. Its predecessor, which dated from 1050AD, was destroyed by the Portuguese but in 1715 a replacement was erected. The *lingam* (sacred phallus) it enshrines is a powerful 'self-born' replica of the one that disappeared in the Portuguese attack. This was held to have been made by Rama himself during his stay, which explains why Walukeshwar attracts followers of both the Vaishnava and Shaivite branches of Hinduism.

North of Malabar Hill

In pre-colonial times, the shoreline immediately north of Malabar Hill used to be submerged under a treacherous tidal creek called the 'Great Breach', which in the first centuries of British rule prevented the northward expansion of the colony. Repeated attempts to close it only served to create a malaria-infested swamp notorious for its 'noxious vapours'. Not until the era of Governor Hornby (1771–84) was an effective sea wall finally built, allowing the flats to be drained and planted.

The rocky outcrop overlooking the Great Breach from the south had for centuries been the site of an ancient Hindu temple, dedicated to the goddess of wealth and prosperity, Mahalakshmi. Pulled down and plundered by marauding Muslims (and, some say, the Portuguese), it had disappeared without trace by the time the British acquired the land. Local legend asserts that the deity enshrined within it appeared to contractors

Tomb of the Sufi mystic Haji Ali

working on the sea defences in the 18th century and told them that the waves would never be restrained unless her image – which she assured them would soon reappear from the sea where it had been thrown by the looters – was reinstated. Sure enough,

> **Before venturing out to Haji Ali's tomb, check high and low tide times in the local newspapers, and avoid the causeway during the monsoons, when waves occasionally wash pilgrims off it.**

a beautiful marble Lakshmi was found in the silt soon after. Installed in a fine new temple, the **Mahalakshmi Temple**, the goddess still flourishes as one of Mumbai's favourites. Devotees queue around the block to present Lakshmi with offerings of huge lotus blooms and silk saris, which the enterprising temple priests recycle from a little shop at the entrance.

Mumbai's most revered Muslim shrine is located a short way further north. Joined to the mainland via a narrow causeway, the **Tomb of Haji Ali** – a Sufi mystic from Afghanistan whose coffin was washed onto the shore after it had been cast into the sea off the coast of Pakistan – occupies a tiny islet in what was once the mouth of the Great Breach. The path to it is only exposed for a few hours at low tide each day, when a steady stream of pilgrims files past the hundreds of beggars, *pirs* (wandering ascetics) and trinket sellers, lining the route, to worship at the shrine. The 19th-century mausoleum itself is a rather tacky affair by the standards of Islamic India; it's best viewed from the promenade across the bay at sunset.

A rather more prosaic spectacle, which (much to the amusement of Mumbaikars) has become a tourist attraction in its own right, are the **Municipal Dhobi Ghats** at the nearby Mahalakshmi railway station. This is where the city's dirty laundry gets a thorough soap and thumping, before being returned to its owners via a network of typical Indian complexity. The nearby railway bridge gives the best vantage point.

CENTRAL MUMBAI

The area of central Mumbai north of Fort and the *maidans*, between Malabar Hill and the docks, is the city's real commercial and popular heart. A densely packed warren of winding streets, wooden galleried *chawls* and markets, it evolved piecemeal over the late-18th and 19th centuries as immigrants poured in from neighbouring states. From wealthy Gujarati merchants to poor Marathi potters and Goan coconut pluckers, each staked out their own quarters, contributing their own brands of architecture, dress and cuisine to the great urban melting pot. These old regional, religious, caste and trade boundaries persist today to a surprising extent. Each of the communities still gravitate around their respective temples or mosques, old residential blocks *(wadis)*, and pillared reception halls *(baugs)* where weddings, feasts and functions are held.

Packed around the main arterial routes running through central Mumbai, the bazaars separate into different streets according to their goods, from flowers and fireworks to carved-stone gods and musical instruments. Navigating your way through the maze can be hard work, but there are plenty of cafés along the way where you can restore your appetite for the pandemonium with a hot *chai*.

Nuts and dry goods in Crawford Market

Crawford Market

Crawford – or **Mahatma Phule** market, as it's officially known these days – is a typically Victorian covered bazaar of a type that will be familiar to British visitors.

Presenting a more sanitised version of the fresh-produce markets uptown, it's where middle-class south Bombay comes to shop for food, household supplies and 'fancy goods' – basically, an Indian-style superstore (only with porters instead of shopping trolleys). An astonishing array of goods are packed into its stalls, ranging from Keralan tender coconuts to Kashmiri saffron, outlandish wigs, prosthetic limbs, aphrodisiac herbs, pet monkeys and flashing electric Ganpati shrines for your car dashboard.

Crawford Market

Only 10 minutes' walk north from CST (VT) station, Crawford Market was built in the 1860s when Rudyard Kipling's father, Lockwood, was the director of the nearby School of Arts. Granite friezes drawn by him, depicting sturdy Indian farmers and smiling mothers with their chubby infants, adorn the main entrance – a vision far removed from the reality of rural life in the late-Victorian period, when tens of millions of poor peasants died of starvation as a direct result of British economic policy. The rest of the exterior combines Swiss, Flemish and Moorish elements, with Tudor-style half-timbered eves and a rather stumpy clock tower.

Inside, the main hall is divided into different sections for fruit, vegetables, nuts and pulses, meats, poultry and dry goods. Under rows of Cordoban arches and wrought-iron lamp brackets in the shape of dragons, its traders perch high up on tiered stalls with their wares spread out in glorious displays below them, bellowing to each other and passers-by. At the rear of the complex, a more anarchic atmosphere prevails in the wholesale section, where porters scurry around with heavy baskets on their heads. The pets' area here is definitely not for the faint hearted.

Kalbadevi

Just across the road from Crawford Market to the north, the mayhem of the bazaar district – **Kalbadevi** – begins in earnest. Congested, noisy and buzzing with life from dawn until an hour or so after dusk, this is the most compelling, intense area of Mumbai – a world away from the open, planned, orderly streets further south. You never quite know what you're going to find around the next corner, and should give up all hope of keeping your sense of direction: just wander until you can't take in any more, then bail out, either by jumping in a taxi, or by asking directions to the district's main arterial route, **Mohammed Ali Road**, where you'll have no difficulty finding transport to other parts of town.

> The streets around the Minara Masjid, at the heart of the Muslim district on Mohammed Ali Road, are converted into an open-air, all-night food festival during Ramadan. Local Muslims congregate here after sunset to break their fasts (*see page 99*).

Silk saris, salwar kameezes and embroidered scarves are the principal stock in trade of the first street north of Crawford Market, **Mangaldas Lane**. Beyond it, the pale-green domes and minarets of the **Jami Masjid** (Friday Mosque) flag the start of Mumbai's sprawling Muslim neighbourhood, where dozens of little mirror-lined shops sell traditional perfumes and exotic *kohl* eye make-up. Follow the main road north from here and you'll eventually end up in **Zaveri**, literally 'silver', a glittering bazaar where locals come to buy their wedding jewellery (still sold by weight).

Further north still, the roads narrow and grow more twisting as you approach Mumbai's most famous temple, **Mumba-Devi**, home of the goddess who is thought to have inspired the name of the city itself. Relocated here from her original shrine, which was destroyed to make way for Victoria Terminus, she now resides under a huge polychrome tower crowned by a gold finial.

Chor Bazaar and 'Grant Road'

A second group of bazaars fan out from Johar Chowk, a couple of kilometres (just over a mile) north of Kalbadevi and Bhuleshwar. Friday morning, the Muslim holy day, is when you should aim to visit the famous **Chor Bazaar** (literally

Fresh fruit in the market

'Thieves Market', though the locals insist its name derives from the Marathi word *shor*, meaning 'noisy'). This is central Mumbai's biggest flea market, where junk, old clothes, cycle parts, *'filmi'* cassettes and all manner of other bric-à-brac from the working neighbourhoods is off-loaded in huge piles – be prepared to rummage and bargain hard. The same applies to the more established shops on **Mutton Road**, which specialise in 'antiques'. Time was when Parsi families, who'd seen better days, would sell off their heirlooms here, but today the market peddles mainly fakes, especially brassy nautical items and forged colonial prints – at inflated prices.

Central Mumbai is packed with dilapidated *chawls* – run-down tenements that have been a feature of life here since the Victorian era. The grim, wood-fronted blocks, with their sagging balconies and collapsing roofs, were originally built by factory owners in the 19th century to house their workers, but have subsequently been inherited by landlords who can no longer afford to maintain them on the low rents they generate. The result is sub-standard housing of a kind, and on a scale, unimaginable in the developed world.

Hemmed in by some of the city's most claustrophobic *chawls*, the red-light district of **Kamathipura**, off Grant Road (now Maulana Shaukatali), is perhaps the most depressing neighbourhood of all. An estimated 25,000 women work here as 'cage girls', plying their trade from tiny barred cells at street level. Many of them are Nepali teenagers sold by their parents into bonded slavery to pay off family debts.

Byculla

The chimney stacks and mills of **Byculla** were the engine room of industrial Bombay during the cotton boom of the late 19th century. With the textile business now based further north, most of the buildings stand forlorn and forgotten – a post-industrial black spot of monumental proportions.

If visitors venture up here at all, it is usually to see the former **Victoria and Albert Museum** – now renamed **Dr Bhau Dadji Lad Museum** (open daily except Wed, 10.30am–4.30pm; admission fee), on Dr BA Road in Byculla-East. When it was opened in 1872, the ornately decorated, Palladian-style pile, set in a classically planned botanical garden, was hailed as 'one of the greatest boons the British have conferred on India'.

Recent renovation work has managed to restore the building to its former glory, but the collection inside falls short of its grand packaging. Among a lacklustre assortment of poorly labelled ceramics, archaeological finds and scale models, the most interesting exhibits are the maps and manuscripts relating to the city's colonial history.

The Victoria and Albert Museum's garden, Byculla

Within the grounds of the museum stands one of the few surviving relics of precolonial Mumbai: the carved stone pachyderm after which Elephanta Island is said to have been named by the Portuguese. It shares the gardens with a handful of dour-looking Victorian statues (among them is one of the Queen Empress herself) which were moved to this location to be beyond the reach of angry mobs upon Independence.

GREATER MUMBAI

A popular distinction has arisen over the past decade or so between 'South Mumbai', characterised by old money and conservative attitudes, and the more affluent suburbs of 'North Mumbai', beyond Mahim Bridge. With their air-conditioned malls and high-rise seafront apartment blocks, Bandra and, to a lesser extent, Juhu, are where the new-money, upwardly mobile classes aspire to live and work, screened from the masses of central Mumbai behind tinted glass and cordons of security guards. If you're only visiting the city, these well-heeled districts can provide much-needed respites

from the chaos further south. They're cleaner, greener and less crowded, the shopping is very much 21st century and the restaurants are a cut above most of those in Colaba.

Bandra

Dubbed the 'Queen of the Suburbs', **Bandra** epitomises the modern, Westernised face of Mumbai. Designer clothes boutiques, trendy cyber cafés and restaurants with valet parking line up along its main thoroughfare, Linking Road (Vithalbhai Patel Marg), all eager to relieve the ranks of hip young things strolling along the pavements of their call centre salaries. It's a far cry indeed from the opposite side of foul-smelling Mahim Creek, on the district's southern flank, which is lined by one of the world's largest slum encampments.

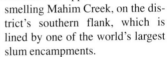

Bandra was first settled by the Portuguese in the 16th century, and remained in their possession well after the rest of the colony had been ceded to the British crown. However, it wasn't until a toll-free causeway joining the island to the rest of Bombay was built (with Parsi money) in 1845 that wealthy citizens started to move up here.

Among the first areas to be extensively settled, a low, sea-facing ridge called **Pali Hill** remains one of modern Mumbai's most exclusive enclaves. And it is now home to scores of millionaire sports celebs,

Bandra, 'Queen of the Suburbs'

On Juhu Beach

Bollywood stars, media tycoons and assorted glitterati.

Bandra's sophisticated food, fashion and nightlife may be what attracts the moneyed classes here, but not even its cool seafront promenade, **Carter Road**, claims a fraction of the traffic that passes through the area en route to the suburb's biggest asset, the **Basilica of Mount Mary**, further south on Land's End.

Worshippers from all of Mumbai's various religious communities – Hindu, Muslim and Parsi – come to this Roman Catholic church, founded by the Portuguese in the 17th century – but substantially rebuilt in the 20th century after a fire – to petition its Madonna, who is believed to possess miraculous powers. Wax models – of body parts, babies and just about anything else that might symbolise a problem or wish – are piled with candles below the statue.

Juhu

Juhu Beach, in the north of the city near the airports, is synonymous in the popular Indian imagination with fun, frolics and easy living. Chances are, if a Bollywood blockbuster in the 1980s included a dance sequence set against a backdrop of seafront five-star hotels or glamorous beachside swimming pools, it will have been filmed here.

Juhu was where the mega-rich and famous of the day let their hair down, giving Mumbai's gossip columnists rich pickings as they were forever reporting the risqué parties going on in its plush apartments. This was also where model and feminist icon Protima Bedi (who later went on to become one of India's finest ever classical dancers) streaked to fame in 1974 in protest against chauvinistic male attitudes to the female body.

The suburb's metamorphosis from remote island to playground for the wealthy started in the 1890s, when the Parsi industrialist Jamsetji Tata (of Taj Mahal Hotel fame) bought land and built a bungalow behind the beach. Other members of the richer classes followed suit, but private attempts to develop the area were stalled by the municipality's refusal to extend the Mahim–Bandra causeway northwards. Not until the 1930s, after Tata flew a Gypsy Moth from Karachi and landed it on the sand flats here (the historic flight that paved the way for Air India and Bombay's airport at nearby Santa Cruz), did international-grade hotels and luxury apartment blocks begin to mushroom.

However, these days, Juhu is less popular with high-living celebrities than it is with ordinary Mumbaikars, who come in their thousands for the fresh air and carnival atmosphere of the beach. At weekends and holidays, the sands swarm with paddlers, cricketers, *bhel-puri wallahs*, troupes of acrobats, dancing monkeys, storytellers, con men, tinsel-covered camels and donkeys offering rides.

In the monsoons of 2005 Juhu was the centre of a mad 'gem rush' after rumours circulated that diamonds had been miraculously washed up on the beach. However, the stones turned out to be merely cut glass fallen off the Ganpati idols that were immersed during the Ganesh Chaturthi festival.

Sanjay Gandhi National Park

Sanjay Gandhi National Park and Kanheri Caves

More than 100 sq km (39 sq miles) of green hillside and forest on the northern edge of Greater Mumbai have been set
aside as the **Sanjay Gandhi National Park**. Encompassing
tracts of teak forest that are miraculously rich in wildlife
considering their proximity to the city, the reserve is a popular retreat from the urban sprawl. It also protects the Kanheri Cave complex, one of Maharashtra's most important
archaeological sites.

Various species of wild deer and antelope inhabit the park,
along with boar, black-faced langur monkeys, and even, it is
alleged, a few wild tigers (though don't come here expecting
to see one). You're more likely to glimpse some of the reserve's flamboyant birdlife: hornbills, junglefowl, golden ori-
oles, kingfishers, bee-eaters and long-tailed drongos all put in
regular appearances. A fenced-off area near to the park's
northern gates, populated by lions, tigers and other animals

rescued from circuses and zoos, can also be visited on child-friendly safaris (daily except Mon, 9am–1pm, 2.30–5pm).

Carved into the sides of a forested valley in the middle of the reserve, the **Kanheri Caves** are much less of a tourist attraction than Elephanta Island but, nevertheless, contain some magnificent ancient sculpture. A total of 109 of them were excavated by Buddhist monks over a 700-year period between the 2nd and 9th centuries AD. They range from simple square cells to elaborately decorated monasteries and *chaitya* halls, linked together by a network of steep, stepped pathways.

It's a good idea to employ one of the guides working at the site to show you around the highlights. These include Cave 2, where Padmapani, the Buddha of Compassion, appears behind a panel showing lines of smaller Buddhas in teaching pose. A *stupa* in this cave bears graffiti neatly carved by one 'N. Christian' in 1810. Two large, serene-faced Buddhas flank the entrance to Cave 3, separated by friezes of heavy-breasted women and their male companions (thought to be flattering depictions of the temple's donors). Carved during the 6th century, Cave 11 is a large monastery hall divided by two long 'tables' that would have been used for unrolling scrolls of Buddhist scriptures. To the left of the entrance, another teaching Buddha is accompanied by some exquisite celestial attendants.

Kanheri Caves, and indeed the Sanjay Gandhi National Park as a whole, are best visited on weekdays; come here on Saturday or Sunday and you'll find the peace and quiet shattered by parties of noisy picnickers.

Kanheri Caves

EXCURSIONS FROM MUMBAI

Mumbai's elongated shape and size mean getting out of the city can sometimes be a challenge – the taxi ride to the airport may take as long as three or four hours if the traffic is bad. That said, with a little advance planning and a few days to spare, some of India's most alluring destinations lie within reach.

Elephanta Island

Several sacred sites around the city's fringes testify to the area's former prominence as a port, but the most awe-inspiring of them is the cave temple at **Elephanta Island**, 9km (6 miles) northeast of the Gateway of India. Hewn from solid basalt at the top of a wooded hill, the shrine is thought to have been created by the Kalachuri dynasty, who ruled most of the Konkan region in the 6th century AD. It contains some of ancient India's finest Hindu sculpture, including a majestic triple-headed Shiva – an image that has become almost as well known as that of Agra's Taj Mahal.

Apart from the Gateway of India, no other Mumbai landmark attracts so many visitors. Be warned, however, that the bulk of them descend on Saturdays and Sundays, when the serenity of the temple can be overwhelmed by noisy crowds, hawkers and troops of aggressive monkeys. To enjoy your trip, therefore, try to avoid weekends.

A fleet of excursion **launches** leaves from the jetty in front of the Gateway of India for the one-hour trip across Mumbai harbour to

Island stop

Elephanta. Tickets can be purchased from the booths in the square. Go for the slightly pricier 'Deluxe' option (Tues–Sun 9am–2.30pm), as you'll be much less cramped and they include the cost of a guide. Grubbier 'Economy' class (Tues–Sun 8am–3pm) boats can get horrendously overloaded. In addition, deluxe ticket holders can return on any service, whereas if you travel economy you'll only be able to come back on an economy launch. The last departure from Elephanta to Mumbai leaves from the island's jetty at 5.30pm.

The 6th–7th century Elephanta temple

Note that no boats sail on Mondays, when Elephanta is closed. Services are also scaled down during the monsoons, and suspended altogether in choppy weather.

Hindu mythology affirms that the **Elephanta cave temple** was the work of the Pandava brothers, whose exploits are recounted in the Hindu epic, the *Mahabharata*. Archaeological evidence, however, suggests more recent origins: probably the late 6th and early 7th centuries AD, at which time the site was known as Gherapuri, or 'Place of Gods'.

Elephanta was the name given to the island by its Portuguese discoverers in the 16th century, after the colossal stone elephant they found on the shoreline (this now resides in the Dr Bhau Dadji Lad Museum in Byculla-East – *see page 59*). The same Portuguese conquistadors inflicted terrible damage on the devotional sculptures they encountered, using some of the deities for target practice. But these depredations have, miraculously, done little to diminish their splendour, which continue to exert a powerful spell on all who stand before them.

Reached via a flight of 100 stone steps, the pillared cave at the top of the island was dedicated to the Hindu god Shiva. Its centrepiece is the famous **Trimurti** (or **Maheshmurti** figure as it's also known), a 6-m (20-ft) tall, triple-headed deity set in an alcove at the back of the cave. Although some debate surrounds the exact date that the figure was carved,

The Trimurti or Maheshmurti

scholars are united in regarding it as the high watermark of ancient Hindu plastic art: no other statue in India emanates such a vivid sense of serenity.

Showing Shiva as Creator, Destroyer and Preserver of the Cosmos, the bust consists of three massive heads. To the left (as you look at it) the god is depicted in his wrathful form as Bhairava, with hooked nose, thick moustache and headdress writhing with cobras. To the right, Vamadeva – Shiva as the Creator – has a softer, more feminine and youthful appearance, wearing flowers in his hair and carrying a lotus bloom. The central image presents Shiva as the Supreme Preserver, Mahadeva, his expression of calm detachment conveying the stillness of eternity. Note the resplendent headdress, coiled dreadlocks and trademark elongated earlobes.

More wonderful sculpture adorns other interior surfaces of the main chamber. Flanking the entrances to a small *lingam* shrine, richly decorated guardian deities sway on either side of the doorways; these bore the brunt of the Portuguese 16th-century fusillade, yet somehow still manage to look serene. Elsewhere on the walls, you'll see other bas-reliefs of Shiva and his associated deities in well-known mythological scenes: the descent of the Ganges to earth through his hair; Shiva's marriage with Parvati; and the dramatic slaying of the demon Andhaka, in which the furious god lunges at his foe with a retributive sword.

> **Elephanta Island is the venue for a colourful music and dance festival organised by the regional tourism corporation, MTDC, each February, in which the floodlit Shiva temple forms the backdrop. Dates and programmes are posted at the India Government Tourist Offices (IGTO) opposite Churchgate Station (*see page 126*).**

Bassein (Vasai)

A century or so before the birth of Bombay as a British trading post, the Portuguese carved out a fully fledged town on the Konkan coast, further north at **Bassein** (or Baçaim as it was then called). Lying on the far banks of the Ulhas River, the evocative ruins of this once-splendid settlement, choked with jungle and almost entirely forgotten, make a pleasant daytrip from the modern city.

A coastal fort was first built on the site by the Sultan of Gujarat, Bahadur Shah, in 1532, but was ceded in perpetuity to the Portuguese only two years later after they took the port of Daman. Preferring not to upset the new European power, with whom it hoped to forge an alliance against the Moghuls, the Sultanate eventually relinquished its claim to the territory and, within a few decades, a flourishing European city sprang up. Disputes between the British and Portuguese over who owned it raged into the late 17th century, however, after the East India Company inherited Bombay through the dowry of Catherine of Braganza. At that time, Baçaim had a population of 60,000 – far greater than the British factory.

Eventually, the matter was settled by the Maratha attack of 1739, in which the Portuguese sustained appalling loss of life. Another bombardment, this time by the British 40 years later, expelled the Marathas, reducing Bassein to a ruinous state from which it never recovered.

Ruins of the Portuguese fort at Bassein

The old ramparts remain intact, but the former Dominican convent, churches and other civic buildings inside have been strangled by creepers and undergrowth, while the quay, where once mighty caravels full of spices would have moored en route to Lisbon, serves a ramshackle local fishing fleet.

To reach Bassein, catch a suburban train from Churchgate Station north to Vasai Road (1 hour), where auto-rickshaws are on hand for the onward ride to the fort (ask for the *Kila*).

Matheran

As the crow flies, only 50km (30 miles) separate Mumbai from its closest hill station, **Matheran**, but it's hard to imagine two more contrasting places. Located at 750m (2,460ft) above sea level, high up on a ridgetop in the Western Ghat mountains, the resort has a cool, salubrious climate, with blissfully fresh air blowing in from the forests and empty hillsides. The site became a popular retreat from the heat of Bombay only after it was surveyed in the 1850s. Pathways were cut soon after to its famous viewpoints – known as 'the Points' – and eventually, a narrow-gauge railway line was laid through the cliffs from the plains below.

With motorised traffic banned from the hill station (everything has to be carried by porters or ponies) and much of the quaint Raj-era architecture still intact, Matheran has retained its original charm. The views from the Points are still as wonderful as they were during British rule, and there are some appealingly old-fashioned hotels where little has changed.

The main incentive to make the trip, however, is the chance to catch the old **toy train** from Neral junction, a rattling 21-km (13-mile), two-hour ride through spectacular mountain scenery. Tickets for the three daily departures (which are timed to link up with the arrival of express trains from Mumbai) may be purchased on spec at Neral, or in advance at the booking hall in Mumbai's CST (VT) station.

Lonavala: Karla and Bhaja

The hill resort of **Lonavala**, on the main highway 120km (74 miles) southeast of Mumbai, is the main jumping-off point for the famous rock-cut caves at Karla and Bhaja. If you found Elephanta Island or Kanheri compelling, then a trip out to these superb historic sites, which hold some of Asia's finest ancient Buddhist architecture, is a must. They can both be reached in a manageable daytrip from Mumbai, though you'll need to employ a taxi or auto-rickshaw driver to transport you between them. As ever, avoid weekends, when the caves are swamped by noisy groups. Guides may be contacted through the IGTO in Churchgate (see page 126).

Excavated around 80BC by Hinayana Buddhist monks, the chaitya hall at **Karla** (open daily 8.30am–sunset; admission fee), 11km (7 miles) from Lonavala along the main NH-4 highway, is the largest and best-preserved of its kind anywhere in India. A long flight of steps climbs more than 100m (330ft) to its excavated courtyard, from which rises an enormous façade dominated by a horseshoe-shaped window. To the left, a tall monolithic pillar sports a capital with four lions, a motif adopted at Independence in 1947 as a symbol of the Indian Republic. Inside, beautifully carved columns capped by elephants and couples run along the sides of the apsidal-ended hall to a large *stupa*. The vaulted ceiling has, astonishingly, retained fragments of perishable teak beams dating from the time when the hall was still in use; they show how the roof was carefully shaped to resemble a wooden structure.

The 18 caves at **Bhaja** (open daily 8.30am–sunset; admission fee) may not be as ornately decorated as Karla's chaitya hall, but they are among the oldest in India, dating from the late 2nd to early 1st century BC. The majority of them are rudimentary *vihara*, or monastic halls, with side verandahs and rows of cells for the monks. One exception is Cave 12, a *chaitya* hall similar in design to the one at nearby

Karla, only with much less ornamentation. Cave 19 harbours some of the earliest examples of figurative art ever discovered in India. Flanking the doorway at one of the verandahs inside, panels depict (on the left) the sun god Surya with two female attendants riding a chariot through the sky; and (on the right) the thunder god Indra astride an elephant, below which you can make out dancers and what looks like a woman with a horse's head.

Entrance to the 80BC *chaitya* hall at Karla

Aurangabad

Buddhist caves carved out of the hillsides that are around **Aurangabad**, 340km (210 miles) northeast of Mumbai, testify to the area's importance in antiquity. However, it wasn't until Malik Amber, the former Abyssinian slave who rose to become prime minister of neighbouring Ahmadnagar state, founded a regional capital, Khirki, here in 1610 that a city took shape on the site. Later, after being sacked by a succession of warlords, the fifth and last great Moghul emperor, Aurangzeb, moved his court to Aurangabad from Agra to supervise his military campaign in the Deccan.

A handful of beautiful mosques and tombs from this era still rise above the dusty modern city, but the reason most visitors come to Aurangabad is to see the world-famous rock-cut caves of Ellora and Ajanta, a daytrip away. From Mumbai's CST (VT) station, you can get here in around seven hours by train, or fly in only 45 minutes. Ranging from palatial five stars to government-run budget hotels, accommodation is plentiful and onward transport to the caves well-organised.

While staying in Aurangabad en route to the caves, it's worth setting aside half a day for the city's own sights. Foremost is the tomb of Aurangzeb's wife, the **Bibi-ka-Maqbara** (open daily 8am–sunset; admission fee), built in 1650–57 by the Emperor's eldest son, Prince Azam Shah. It stands on the outskirts, set against a dramatic backdrop of desert escarpments. Critics over the centuries have poured scorn on the mausoleum and its ornamental walled gardens for being a squat, ill-proportioned copy of the Taj Mahal. But this fails to do justice to the Bibi-ka-Maqbara's very fine ornamentation, most of which survives. Standing on a raised

Bibi-ka-Maqbara

plinth with octagonal minarets on all four corners, the domed tomb rises above an inner vault enclosed behind finely carved marble lattice screens. The unmarked, open-topped grave of the Empress Rabi'a Diwani lies in stark contrast to its sumptuous surroundings.

High on the basalt hillside overlooking the tomb are two small, but historically important groups of **rock-cut caves** (open Tues–Sun 8.30am–5pm; admission fee), around 1km (just under a mile) apart. The earliest – a rectangular *chaitya* hall (Cave 4) very similar to those at Karla and Bhaja – dates from the Satavahana period in the 1st century AD. Its neighbour, Cave 3, the largest of the western group, contains some remarkable early sculpture showing devotees kneeling before a preaching Buddha. Cave 7, the pick of the other, eastern group, holds an impressive panel of six goddesses and depictions of the Bodhisatvas, with attendants and flying celestials flanking the doorway into the main sanctuary.

Ellora

The rock-cut caves at **Ellora**, 29km (18 miles) away from Aurangabad, have astonished travellers since their rediscovery in the late 17th century. Few of the many visitors who make the long journey up here from Mumbai are prepared for the awesome scale of the site, nor the wealth of ancient art it contains. Hewn from solid basalt, a total of 34 separate cave complexes honeycomb the 2-km (1-mile plus) long Chanadiri escarpment, covering a 500-year period that began in the 6th century AD – roughly when the occupation of Ajanta was petering out.

Quite why the local rulers chose this remote spot is a matter of speculation, but the proximity of the region's main trade artery, linking the great cities of central India with the ports of the west coast, is thought to be key. Taxes from the through trade would have provided the region's ruling dynasties – the

Ellora rock-cut caves are on an awesome scale

Chalukyas and Rashtrakutas – with the funds they needed to finance the excavations, which achieved their apogee with the mighty Kailash Temple, Ellora's world-famous masterpiece, hewn from the hillside in the 8th century.

Unlike Ajanta, the Chanadiri cliff did not escape the iconoclasm of the Muslim era, and sustained considerable damage – the worst of it ordered by the Moghul Emperor Aurangzeb himself who, in a fit of zeal reminiscent of the Taliban's 2002 destruction of the Bamian Buddhas in Afghanistan, ordered the demolition of Ellora's 'heathen idols'. Numerous scars remain from this time, but the bulk of the site's sculpture looks remarkably fresh and vital.

The caves are numbered from south to north, starting with the oldest Buddhist ones, cut between AD500 and 700. From around 600, Hinduism began to gain the upper hand and prevailed until the local kings adopted Jainism in the late 9th and 10th centuries. A small cluster of caves at the northern edge of the escarpment dates from this period.

It's definitely worth hiring one of the official guides who work at Ellora to show you around. If time is short, concentrate on Cave 6, whose antechamber holds two especially fine figures of Tara and Mahamayuri, and Cave 10, one of the most magnificent of all the Deccan's early Buddhist *chaitya* halls.

Leave the Kailash temple, in the middle of the site (open daily 8.30am–sunset; admission fee), until the end of the afternoon, when the longer shadows bring the ornate carvings into relief. Commissioned by the Rashtrakuta King Krishna 1 (AD756–773), Kailash is not so much a cave as a vast monolith carved in imitation of the free-standing temples being erected in the south of India at that time. Around a quarter of a million tons of material are thought to have been chiselled out of the hillside to make the complex, which was conceived as a representation of Mount Kailash, Shiva's 'Divine Axis' joining heaven and earth. Originally, its elaborately carved surfaces would have been plastered in a snow-like

Carvings at Ellora

coat of lime plaster, patches of which still remain in places. As well as representing a mountain, the temple also symbolises Shiva's chariot, complete with giant wheels and a pair of (now badly disfigured) elephants to haul it along. Superb friezes and panels of mythological sculpture, much of it violent or erotic, adorn the exterior surfaces. The finest of all is one on the side of the *mandapa* hall showing Shiva and his consort Parvati being disturbed in their celestial abode by the multi-headed devil Ravana; Shiva is about to calm the earthquake with a prod of his cosmic toe, as Parvati, reclining on her elbow, looks nonchalantly on.

Ajanta

'The finest gallery of pictures to survive from any ancient civilisation' is how the historian John Keay classified the **Ajanta caves**. No other body of classical art in the world, not even that of Greece, Egypt or the Aztecs, yields such a vivid, naturalistic and comprehensive view of a lost society. Adorning walls that were cut from solid rock, the fresco paintings – or *tempera* as they should more accurately be described – are all the more remarkable for being almost perfectly preserved, their colours still vibrant and details crisp. The reason for this is the site's extreme remoteness.

Lost deep in the Deccan mountains, on the margins of what was British territory and that of the Nizam of Hyderabad, the caves were hollowed out of a sweeping U-shaped ravine whose existence was known only to aboriginal Bhils until 1824, when a young British officer, Lieutenant James Alexander of the 16th Bengal Lancers, stumbled upon them during a tiger hunt.

His discovery proved to be one of the most sensational archaeological finds of all time. A total of 28 pillared halls had been carved out of Ajanta's basalt cliffs, many of them decorated inside with resplendent murals.

As the caves' fame spread, more people began to travel here to see them and today Ajanta, despite its far-flung location,

---

The Ajanta Curse

Early attempts to document the Ajanta excavations to show them to a wider world were bedevilled by a string of uncanny setbacks, which the press at the time likened to the curse of Tutankhamun. In 1866, the artist Robert Gill, who had spent 27 years painting facsimiles at the site, lost his entire collection in the Crystal Palace fire. Undeterred, he started again, but died soon after in India. A second set of reproductions were incinerated when the Royal Victoria and Albert Museum exhibiting them burned down (though these had been photographed). And a third batch, painted on rice paper by Japanese artists, was lost in an earthquake.

Restoration work in later decades was also dogged with disaster. Italian picture restorers employed by the Nizam of Hyderabad to preserve the paintings nearly destroyed them after they covered them with a protective coat of varnish. Over time this darkened, cracked and flaked, pulling patches of paint away. Much of the damage has been made good, but you can still see sections that have been ruined for ever.

These days, the job of looking after Ajanta, and ensuring that the breath and camera flashes from the thousands of visitors who stream through the caves each week doesn't further deteriorate the paintwork, falls to the Archaeological Survey of India (ASI).

ranks among India's most visited monuments. Entrance to the site (open daily 9am–5.30pm; admission fee) is strictly controlled by the Archaeological Survey of India (ASI). You can either join a group tour or employ your own guide; either way, you'll need some help to interpret the enigmatic art and its historical context.

Cave excavation at Ajanta spanned 700 or 800 years, beginning in the 2nd century BC. Small communities of Buddhist monks used to shelter in the ravine during the monsoon rains, and over the years this seasonal settlement coalesced into permanent monasteries that grew progressively more ambitious in scale and design. At the height of its popularity, around 200 monks would probably have lived here, as well as a legion of painters, sculptors, labourers, cooks, servants and pilgrims passing through. No one is exactly sure why the complex went into decline, but the rise of Hinduism and the rival site of Ellora are the most likely culprits. Whatever the cause of Ajanta's demise, it's amazing to think such a storehouse of exquisite art could, over time, be so forgotten.

Following the caves in chronological order, it is possible to chart the evolution of Buddhist iconography in India from its comparatively austere, restrained beginnings under the Hinayana School, to the exuberant, Hindu-influenced Mahayana era, by which time the simply sculpted *chaitya* halls of the early period had been superseded by huge rectangular *vihanas* with lavishly painted interiors.

Drawing on the stories associated with the Buddha's various incarnations (the *jatakas*), Ajanta's murals incorporate a wonderful array of subject matter, from royal seraglios and almond-eyed princesses dripping in finery to child-eating ogres, jungles, religious processions, school rooms, shipwrecks, mourners, flying angels, rampant elephants and monkey troops – in short, an entire ancient world in microcosm. They were painted on to panels made from a paste of dried clay, cow dung and animal hair, and finished with a skim coat of limewash. Over this, the artists applied their pigments, ground from a variety of minerals such as lamp soot (black), glauconite (green), ochre (yellow) and Afghan lapis lazuli (blue).

Each of the caves has its own special masterpieces, and you could spend days or weeks pouring over any of them. One image, however, encapsulates the spirit of Ajanta's sublime art more completely than perhaps any other. In Cave 1, to the left of the doorway leading to the main shrine, the Bodhisattva Avalokiteshvara in the form of Padmapani is shown delicately holding a lotus flower. Despite being surrounded by an entourage of celestial musicians, playful apes and all manner of other distractions, he exudes a mood of profound inner calm – the perfect embodiment of the Buddhist concept of enlightened compassion.

The Ajanta caves are a storehouse of exquisite art

आई एकवीरिचा उदो उदो

कथा/पटकथा/संवाद
आणि दिग्दर्शन
राजू फुलकर

संगीत
प्रसाद-अद्वैत

छाया
नंदकुम

WHAT TO DO

ENTERTAINMENT

What Mumbai may lack in monuments, it certainly makes up for with entertainment options. Movie-going is without doubt the city's favourite pastime and you'd be missing out if you didn't take in at least one Hindi block-buster during your visit. Art galleries and theatres further enhance local cultural life, and for those wishing to see how the smart set party, Mumbai's bars and nightclubs rank among some of the most sophisticated in Asia.

Cinema

Between half and three-quarters of a million cinema tickets are sold each week in Mumbai, depending on the popularity of the latest offering from the city's own record-beating film industry, Bollywood. For the definitive *'filmi'* experience, go to one of the wonderful 1930s' Art Deco cinemas in the centre of town: the Eros, opposite Churchgate Station; the Metro, at the top of Azad Maidan/MG Road, on Dhobi Talao; or the Regal, at the top of SBS Marg in Colaba. All three boast state-of-the-art surround sound and projection, are well air-conditioned and have comfortable seats, although, as with all Indian movie houses, things can get a bit rowdy down in the stalls, with leering, shouting, dancing in the aisles and baddies being pelted with peanuts – a spectacle much better enjoyed from the relative safety of the upstairs circle.

To avoid the pre-screening rush, tickets are best purchased well in advance from the box office. You can find out what's on, and where, in any local newspaper. Alternatively, take your chances and pick a film on the strength of its hoarding.

A Bollywood film hoarding

Bollywood

Playing to audiences of around 14 million every day, India's film industry is the biggest in the world, far outstripping even Hollywood (in terms of ticket sales if not actual box-office receipts). Close on 1,000 movies are released in the country annually, half of them from the Bollywood studios of north Mumbai – home of the Pan-Indian, Hindi-language blockbuster. It's impossible to escape the city's love affair with the 'talkies' (as the movies are sometimes still referred to). Images of the current stars are ubiquitous. You'll see them wherever boredom might need to be alleviated: from the giant hoardings that loom above traffic jams, to video screens on station platforms.

The cipher behind the phenomenal success of the Bollywood blockbuster is the so-called 'masala' (literally 'spice') format. Since its infancy in the late 1960s, directors have realised that to appeal to the masses in villages across the country, movies had to include a little (or a lot) of everything: high melodrama, comedy, violence, music, dance, striking outfits and lashings of romance. Plots thus tend to pursue familiar lines, usually involving a maverick 'hero' who battles with injustice and, against all odds, wins through to marry the girl he loves. Religious piety versus moral degeneracy, and the break up and reunion of a family are other essential themes. And you'll always get a supporting cast of stock characters such as the comic villain, loose woman (wearing Western clothes), corrupt priest or politician, and evil moneylender.

At the heart of this colour-saturated maelstrom will, of course, be the love story. In a country where marriages are nearly always brokered by relatives instead of based on sexual attraction, romance is guaranteed to cast a potent spell, which is why your average big-budget Bollywood flick includes at least half-a-dozen love song sequences. Swirling through as many different costume changes as exotic locations, these might switch from a Kashmiri meadow or Keralan rice field, to a Goan beach or Rajput palace, before cutting to a Swiss lake or London's Tower Bridge. But because Indian censorship laws forbid touching lips, the lovers never (quite) get to kiss – though they might get to roll around flower-filled Alpine meadows or Nilgiri tea gardens, enjoy plenty of hip-thrusting disco dances and cavort in skimpy clothes through monsoon rainstorms.

The tried-and-tested masala format has seen challenges in recent years, following the success of crossover hits such as *Lagaan* and *Bride & Prejudice*. These films may not sell as many tickets in the Indian provinces, but they fill cinemas in Southall and New Jersey, where tickets cost 10 times what they do back home. As a result, less stylised acting, more foreign locations, multi-star casts and much smaller miniskirts have started to creep into Bollywood.

Traditional dancer

Performing Arts

For nearly four decades, the prime venue in Mumbai for music recitals, dance and drama has been the **National Centre for the Performing Arts**, on Nariman Point in the far south of the city. It was set up (as ever, by Parsi benefactors) in the mid-1960s to preserve and promote India's traditional cultural legacy and hosts a constantly revolving programme of events. This is where you're most likely to catch one of the country's top classical musicians in action – whether Carnatic (from the south) or Hindustani (from the north) – as well as recitals of dance forms such as Bharatiya Natyam, Kathak and Odissi. Troupes of folk musicians and dancers from across India also put in regular appearances here, as do puppeteers, traditional regional-language theatre groups, and exponents of various ritual traditions, from Kathakali to Teyyem.

Nightlife

Mumbai's nightlife is legendary in India. Being seen at the hippest parties in the most fashionable designer clothes is very much an essential part of being rich and famous in a city that idolises wealth and fame. The relentless pursuit of celebrities by gossip magazines only serves to fuel the fascination for Mumbai's bright lights.

Clubbing in Mumbai

Attitudes to alcohol have always been more liberal than elsewhere in the country. As a result, Mumbai's **bars** tend to be relaxed, and less like the curtained dens of moral degeneracy they are in other Indian towns and cities. Even women can enjoy a beer (at least, in the more sophisticated places) without disapproving stares, though you can expect plenty of unwanted attention if you try drinking it at the bar on your own.

Some of Mumbai's most appealing bars are located down in Colaba: try the famous Café Mondegar on SBS Marg, which sells draught Pilsner by the glass or pitcher, or Leo's Square, above the popular Leopold Café, further down the same street. For a glimpse of the city's *beau monde* at their air-kissing best, the place to go is Indigo, at 4 Mandlik Marg, also in Colaba, whose minimalist decor redefined 'funky' when it first appeared on the scene a decade or so ago *(see Recommended Restaurants on page 137)*.

A recent international bestseller set in modern Mumbai, describing life in the city from the perspective of its slums and underworld, is Gregory David Robert's *Shantaram*. For a compelling non-fiction account of the metropolis, read Suketu Mehta's award-winning *Maximum City*.

Nightclubs tend to be rather less laid-back than bars, not least because the very idea of men and women grooving away together on a dance floor flies in the face of Indian cultural norms. That said, today's 20-somethings behave in pretty much the same way as they would in London or New York, albeit in a rather more rarefied atmosphere. With entrance charges higher than the average monthly wage of a manual worker from uptown, the city's clubs are the exclusive preserve of its wealthiest society.

Club music tends to be a mix of the latest R&B, hip hop and house, with a few crowd-pleasing Hindi pop numbers thrown in. Downtown, Athena in Colaba is the most renowned of Mumbai's nightspots, along with Insomnia, which is located in the basement of the nearby Taj Mahal Palace and Tower Hotel. Polly Esther's, in Colaba's Gorden House Hotel on Battery Street, is another hot tip, with regular theme nights and fun retro decor.

SHOPPING

It's probably fair to say that at street level in Mumbai you can't ever be more than 10 paces away from somebody selling something. Aside from all the regional handicrafts and other homespun produce you'd expect to find in any major Indian city, the shops along Colaba's SBS Road, and in the swisher suburb of Bandra, sell the latest fashions – from jeans to sportswear – at much lower prices than in Europe or North America. Larger and more established places, such as trendy clothes stores and government shops, offer fixed prices and will accept credit and debit cards, but in more traditional outlets you'll have to haggle out a price and pay in cash.

Souvenirs. A good place to start any hunt for souvenirs is the **Central Cottage Industries Emporium** on Shivaji Marg in Colaba, just down the road from the Gateway of India. A

Shopping for souvenirs

government-run store that specialises in high-quality, regionally produced handicrafts, it is especially strong on textiles, including Rajasthani mirrorwork, Gujarati appliqué, Kanchipuram saris

> **Bear in mind when shopping for souvenirs that it is illegal to export from India any object that is more than 100 years old.**

and Orissan ikat weave, as well as metal- and woodwork.

Textiles. More traditional Indian textiles, sold off the roll or as ready-made garments, are offered across town at the **Khadi Village Industries Emporium** on DN Marg, near Thomas Cook. Hand-spun silk and cotton are its main stock, but you can also pick up bargain sandalwood items and *dhurrie* rugs, often at amazing discounts. The emporium was set up in Gandhi's time to promote the village-made goods he regarded as essential to Indian '*swaraj*', or 'home rule', and little has changed since. The packaging of goods, not to mention payment, involves a cast of a dozen or so slow-moving employees.

Antiques. Indian law regulates the sale of objects more than 100 years old, but this has done little over the years to dent the trade of **Phillip's Antiques**, opposite the Regal Cinema in Colaba. A period piece in itself, the shop, adorned with wooden fixtures and glass cases, sells a fascinating assortment of mainly Raj-era maps, prints and *objets d'art*.

Bazaars. Also worth a browse are the market areas in the heart of the city *(see pages 54–8)*, although you'll need a good inner compass and plenty of stamina to do them justice. Grouped around the Minara Mosque on Mohammed Ali Road, look out for the tiny **Muslim perfumeries**, with their cut-glass bottles full of exotic perfumes whose secret recipes have been passed down from father to son for generations.

Books. Bookworms are spoiled for choice in Mumbai. Outside the Café Mondegar in Colaba, the tiny **Strand Book**

Stall has been furnishing travellers with reading matter for decades, and this is where you'll find all the classics of Indian fiction, travel writing and religion in paperback. The air-conditioned **Oxford Bookstore** on Dinsha Vaccha Road, off Oval Maidan, has an even more impressive selection, with the bonus of a pleasant coffee shop attached *(see page 141)*. If you don't find what you're looking for there, try **Nalanda** on the ground floor of the Taj Mahal Palace and Tower.

Laughter Clubs

Take an early-morning jog along Juhu Beach *(see page 62)* and you'll be treated to one of Mumbai's more hilarious spectacles: groups of mostly middle-aged people standing in semi-circles with their hands in the air, laughing their heads off for apparently no reason. As it turns out, 'laughter clubs' are a lot more serious than they look. They are part of a new therapy known as *lasya yoga*, devised in 1995 by a Mumbai doctor, Madan Kataria, and his wife Madhuri – aka 'the Giggling Gurus'. The Katarias experimented with the yogic principle that there's nothing better for the soul than a good guffaw, and found that if you laugh for 15–20 minutes each morning you remain 'charged with happiness' for the rest of the day.

Sessions follow a strict pattern, starting with rhythmic clapping and chanting of 'ho ho ha ha'. From there, participants progress to 'hearty laughter' ('Raise both hands in the air with the head tilting backwards'), 'milkshake laughter' ('Everyone laughs while making a gesture as if they are drinking milkshake') and 'swinging laughter' ('Stand in a circle saying aaee oo eee uuu') before the rather terrifying 'lion laughter' ('Extrude the tongue fully with eyes wide open and hands stretched out like claws, and laugh from tummy'). The session then winds up with holding hands and the chanting of slogans ('We are the laughter club member (sic) . . . Y . . . E . . . S!').

For the full story, visit <www.laughteryoga.org>.

SPORTS

In a country as obsessed with cricket as India, few other spectator sports stand much of a chance. However, Mumbai does boast one of the most famous horse racing courses in the country, where the ruling elite love to hobnob, just as in British times. The working classes, meanwhile, watch the more

Born to bat

traditional Indian sports of *kabaadi* and *kushti* wrestling in neighbourhood parks.

Details of all forthcoming sporting events are posted in the back pages of the Mumbai edition of the *Times of India*.

Cricket

Indians are crazy about cricket, and Mumbaikars are no exception. One of the city's most picturesque spectacles are the matches held each day on Oval and Azad Maidans, in front of the old Victorian buildings of Kala Ghoda and Fort. These might range from formal club games in full whites to impromptu knockabouts, but they're all played to an amazingly high standard.

Amateur matches on the maidans, or at the gymkhanas on Marine Drive, can be enjoyable diversions. For the full-on Indian cricket experience, however, you should try to catch a first-division or test game at the **Wankhede**, India's largest stadium, near Churchgate Station. Fans used to the more sedate atmosphere of British or Antipodean terraces will understand why visiting players find the atmosphere at Wankhede as intimidating as any test venue in the world. Up to 45,000

Mahalakshmi Race Course

spectactors may be crammed into it on any given day, roaring, chanting and lighting crackers. The mayhem is all extremely good natured, though, and as a visiting cricket fan you'll be greeted with great enthusiasm. Mumbaikars love to talk about the game, so don't be surprised if you get drawn into a highly technical conversation by someone who knows your team's batting and bowling averages better than you do.

The Indian cricket season runs from October until the end of February. Tickets for Wankhede matches can be bought at the main gates on D Road, of Marine Drive. Seats for major tests tend to be at a premium, but visitors can sometimes access special quotas through the Mumbai Cricket Association on the first floor of the stadium.

Further south down Marine Drive is the shabbier **Brabourne Stadium**, home of the venerable Cricket Club of India where the likes of Sunil Gavaskar and Sachin Tendulkar cut their teeth.

Horse Racing and Riding

The **Mahalakshmi Race Course**, near the Mahalakshmi Temple just north of Malabar Hill, is the home of the Royal Western India Turf Club – a throwback to British days that still flourishes as a social venue for the city's elite. Meetings are held twice weekly, on Wednesdays and Saturdays, between November and March. Big races attract the cream of the country's racing fraternity, with crowds of around 25,000. Entrance to the public ground is by normal ticket, purchased at the gates on the day, but seats in the elegant Raj-era stand, with its posh lawns and restaurant, is restricted to members (though with a letter of introduction from your hotel or a business associate, smartly dressed visitors will usually be granted permission for a one-off entry). Race cards for Mahalakshmi meets are posted in the back pages of the *Times of India*, along with form guides, or you can download them from the club's website at <www.rwitc.com>.

When it's not hosting races, Mahalakshmi serves as the grounds of the **Amateur Riding Club of Mumbai**, whose members include famous film stars and billionaires. Temporary membership, entitling you to use the club's beautiful horses for gentle early-morning hacks around the course, is offered to visitors (full details on <www.arcmumbai.com>).

Kabaadi and Kushti

Mentioned in ancient Hindu texts such as the Mahabharata, *Kabaadi* is a traditional sport that's still immensely popular throughout South Asia. Two teams face each other from either side of a level court; a raider from one enters the other's half and attempts to tag or wrestle to the ground a member of the opposite team while holding their breath and chanting '*kabaadikabaadikabaadi…*' (to show they're not cheating). The defending team, meanwhile, tries to grab the raider to prevent him or her from returning to their end of the pitch

EATING OUT

Mumbai is, quite simply, a foody's paradise. Whatever budget you're travelling on, you'll be able to enjoy freshly cooked, skilfully prepared dishes, full of exotic flavours and ingredients, on virtually every street corner. Ranging from strictly vegetarian South Indian to rich, meat-based Mughali cooking from the north of the country, diverse cuisines have been brought here by immigrant communities from all over India and pitched in to the city's gastronomic melting pot. In each case – whether Gujarati, Konkani, Parsi or Chinese – certain restaurants have emerged over the years as definitive, and one of the best ways of getting to know Mumbai is to travel between them, sampling their respective signature dishes and distinctive atmosphere.

Of course, as well as the established places, there are also trendy new restaurants serving whatever kind of food is currently in fashion: Italian, Thai or 'Indian-fusion'. Such restaurants tend to come and go and change chefs more often than at traditional ones. However, with competition rife, standards of cooking are high and, compared with most European and North American countries, you get amazing value.

Snacks

In such a fast-paced city, quick snacks are a major part of street life. Wander around the 'Khau Gullies' (literally 'eating lanes') of Fort or Churchgate at lunchtime or just after offices close, and you'll see literally thousands of workers at mobile stalls tucking into little plates of Mumbai-style fast food to steel themselves for the sweaty, cramped train journey home. **Pao bhaji** – a spicy tomato and red-lentil mush cooked with butter and served sprinkled with finely chopped coriander in a fluffy white roll – is the commuters' favourite.

Pao Bhaji, a red lentil mush, with pitta bread and dips

Hot, spicy, filling and cheap, it's served from giant iron skillets which vendors drum with their spatulas to advertise their presence to passers-by.

The other quintessentially Mumbai snack you'll see everywhere is **bhel puri** – a scrumptious heap of puffed rice, deep-fried vermicelli, potato and crunchy pieces of *puri* (flat bread) mixed with chopped tomatoes, raw onions, fresh coriander, a twist of tamarind and lemon juice. *Bhel puri* is served in quite a few proper restaurants and cafés (notably the famous Vithal Bhelwalla near CST (VT) station – *see page 140*), but you'll come across it more frequently at (less hygienic) wheelie stalls, especially on Chowpatty and Juhu beaches.

Restaurants and Cuisines

Although most restaurants in Mumbai typically offer a huge range of dishes (Indian, Chinese and Continental), the

Restaurant overlooking the Gateway of India

chances are that they'll specialise in only a handful, and that's what all the locals will be eating.

For a quick sit-down pit-stop, the most popular option has to be the **udipi**, or South Indian snack canteen – named after the Hindu pilgrimage town of Udipi in southern Karnataka, where many of the dishes originated. Simple, no-frills places staffed by a legion of kitchen boys in cotton overalls and more snappily shirted waiters, they are nearly always scrupulously vegetarian (which means no eggs or fish, let alone meat).

At **lunchtime** *udipis* offer copious set meals or **thalis**, consisting of half a dozen different spicy vegetable dishes and lentil stews *(dals)*, accompanied by rice, pappadams, yoghurt *(raita)* and a blob or two of pickle *(achar)* and *chatnis*, all placed in stainless-steel cups on large round tin trays (the eponymous *thali*). Portions are usually 'unlimited' – i.e. the boys patrol the canteen and spoon refills on to any meal which looks like it's getting smaller.

For **breakfast** and throughout the day, *udipis* also serve steamed rice cakes, or *idlys*, with deep-fried, round *wada* doughnuts made from maize flour. These come with small servings of coconut-based *chatni* and a tangy, hot lentil sauce flavoured with tamarind, called *sambar*.

Chatni-sambar is also the standard accompaniment for the most famous of all *udipi* snacks, the *dosa* – huge, circular pancakes made from fermented rice-flour batter that's fried on a hot griddle plate and rolled into a huge tube. When stuffed with a mix of potato, onions, chopped green chillies, pieces of coconut and mustard seeds, it becomes a more substantial *masala dosa* – a wonderfully tasty meal in itself.

No two *dosas* will ever be the same and every Mumbaikar has his or her favourite joint and particular style of preparation. *Dosas* can come with a variety of fillings, a drizzle of *ghee* (clarified butter), wafer thin or thick. The batter may also be blended with finely chopped onions and poured in cross-hatched diagonal lines on to the griddle, rather than spread into a round pancake, to make a crunchier *rawa masala dosa*.

Other *udipi* standards include *uttapams*, which are made from a similar kind of batter as *dosas*, but fried in thicker, smaller round pancakes. With the addition of chopped onions, green chillies, tomatoes and a layer of grated Western-style cheese, they make India's version of the pizza – the cheese *uttapam*.

Konkan cuisine (also known as Mangalorean), from coastal southwest India, is a non-vegetarian, essentially domestic

The Ramadan Night Market

Any visitor finding themselves in Mumbai during the Muslim month of Ramadan shouldn't miss the wonderful night market ranged around the Minara Masjid on Mohammed Ali Road. After sunset, the locals break their fasts with meals of traditional festival food – *sheesh kebabs*, *rumali rotis*, fried kidneys, *baida* (egg) *parathas* and mutton curries – whipped up at lines of brightly lit street stalls. For dessert, try *saviya ki kher* – vermicelli simmered in milk and sugar, and garnished with pistachios and almonds.

version of *udipi* cooking. It depends heavily on seafood: tiger prawns, crab, clams and fish such as snapper, pomfret, barramundi and shark steak, fillets of which are either simmered in fiery stews based on coconut milk, sour *kokum* juice, tamarind water and chillies – the famous *gassi* – or else steamed in banana leaves. Either way the results are sublime. Instead of wheat *chappatis*, the standard accompaniment for Konkani *gassi* are *appams*, pikelets of fermented rice-flour batter which steam when you rip them open; they sometimes have a slightly sour, smoky flavour imparted by coconut sap, or *toddi*.

Mumbai's best Konkan restaurants (Trishna, Apoorva and the Mahesh Seafood Home – *see Restaurant Listings starting on page 136*) are where you're most likely to find the

Irani Cafés

Around the turn of the 20th century, a second wave of Zoroastrian immigrants from Iran settled in Mumbai (more than 300 years after the first Parsis arrived in the city from Gujarat). Many opened small cafés, decorating them in distinguished *fin de siècle* style, with wood panelling, bevelled-edge mirrors, bentwood chairs and marble table tops. Bombayites from all walks of life used to congregate in these so-called Irani cafés over little china cups of strong, sweet tea and plates of *bun maska* (white buttered bread rolls, warmed on a griddle), and over time they became a much-loved feature of life in the city. But the past two or three decades have seen many of them close, or modernise into trendier beer bars. A handful of old-style stalwarts, however, remain as evocative reminders of this lost era, their decor and menus barely altered since the 1920s. Two of the best are Kyani's (also known as the House of Cakes), near the Metro Cinema at Dhobi Talao, and Yezdani's Bakery, in Cowasji Patel Street, Fort. In Colaba, the wonderful Olympia Coffee House serves traditional Mughlai-style Muslim food in a superbly well-preserved Irani dining hall.

city's speciality, Bombay Duck *(see page 45)*. It's not duck but, in fact, a kind of dried fish that may be prepared in a variety of ways, but is most often rolled in turmeric batter and eaten with piping hot *appam*.

From the opposite side of India, **Mughlai** cuisine takes its cue from the elaborate style of cooking that was favoured by the sybaritic Moghul emperors. The intermingling of Hindu India's love of spices with the Per-

An Irani Café

sian and Afghan invaders' predilection for saffron, nuts and dried fruit gave rise to dishes famed for their delicate flavours and rich, creamy sauces. Chicken and mutton form the basis for most of them, but fresh vegetables and pulses are also extensively used. Again, no two restaurants ever seem to serve the same version of any given dish, jealously guarding recipes and passing them on from generation to generation.

Mughlai cooking also gave the world the *tandoor* clay oven, used to quick-bake the kind of kebabs, *tikka* and *naan* breads enjoyed in curry houses throughout the West – only in Mumbai they're deployed to considerably greater effect by specialist *tandoori* chefs, using coatings of spice pastes and superb yoghurt-based sauces.

For authentic, Persian-inflected north Indian cuisine, it's worth splashing out on a meal at one of the classier Mughlai restaurants in the city such as the Khyber in Kala Ghoda *(see page 137)*. But there are also plenty of other reputed Muslim eateries serving more everyday (but no less tasty) food, albeit in rather less ostentatious surroundings. Well-heeled families from south Mumbai love to rough it at streetside *kebab-wallahs* such as the famous **Bade Miyan** behind the Taj, which rustles up flame-grilled chicken, lamb *sheesh kebabs* and paper-thin *rotis* – huge round flatbreads baked in a matter of seconds on a dome-shaped griddle.

Another immigrant community that brought its recipes from Persia and adapted them with Indian ingredients were the Parsis, or Zoroastrians. **Parsi** dishes are distinguished by their complex textures and mixing of nuts, apricots, hot chutneys and vinegar. Mutton *dhansak*, a combination of brown rice and different pulses with aubergine (eggplant), tamarind and a distinctive blend of spices, is the hallmark Parsi dish, traditionally eaten at Sunday lunch.

On grander occasions such as weddings, *patra ni machi* is more often served – slices of fish, such as pomfret, coated with green chutney, wrapped and steamed in banana leaves. Only a handful of Parsi restaurants survive where you can eat authentic dishes such as these, the best of them being Britannia in Ballard Estate, Jimmy Boy near Horniman Circle and Ideal Corner in Fort *(see page 139)*.

Drinks

Tea – or *chai* – is India's national drink and in Mumbai, as elsewhere in the country, it's drunk strong, milky and sweet in tiny cups or glasses. Everyday *chai* tends to be made from granulated or powdered, low-grade leaves (a product known as CTC – cut, trimmed and curled). But you can sample fine tea in its more full, subtle and aromatic, 'withered-leaf' form at upscale teahouses such as the famous Tea Centre on VN Road *(see page 141)*.

India also produces high-quality **coffee** and since the cappuccino boom in the West lots of trendy Starbucks-style coffee shops have opened in Mumbai. These make a much more flavoursome product than what you'd typically find at a more run-of-the-mill Indian refreshments stall on station platforms and street corners, where the coffee will be instant, milky and sweet – in fact, much like *chai*.

To quench the monster thirsts that easily mount while exploring the city, **bottled water**, available chilled in corner shops and stalls everywhere, is the safest option – just make sure the plastic seal on the top is intact. Coke, Pepsi, Seven Up and a variety of Indian soft

Tea time

drinks (including Thumbs Up cola, Limca lemonade and Gold Spot orange pop) are also readily available. And **juice** bars – serving freshly squeezed orange, pineapple, *chickoo* (sapodilla) and pomegranate – are common. Most are hygienic enough, but make sure your drink comes with no ice (which will be made from less reliable tap water).

Attitudes towards **alcoholic drinks** are much more liberal in Mumbai than other parts of India. Many bars and cafés serve beer, often proper draught by the pint, which usually contains less glycerine (used as a preservative) than the bottled variety. Spirits tend to be available only in hotels and late-night bars. All but the most expensive are IMFL (Indian Made Foreign Liquor) which tend to be consumed with a mixer.

Wine has only quite recently started to gain in popularity among India's affluent middle classes. Produced in a handful of vineyards in the temperate uplands of the Western Ghat mountains and Deccan Plateau, it's rarely as good as what you can buy at the same prices abroad, but quality seems to be increasing with each vintage. The three most dependable labels to look out for are Grover's, Sula and Château Indage.

To Help You Order...

I want (a masala dosa).	**Mujhe (masala dosa) chahiye.**
Is it possible?	**Kya ye sambhav hai?**
How much (money)?	**Kitna paise hai?**
That's expensive.	**Bahut mahenga hai.**
thank you	**dhanyavad/shukriya**

Cocktails or fruit juice from the bar

cheap	**sasta**	hot	**garam**
without chilli	**mirch ke bina**	cold	**tanda**
without sugar	**cheeni nehin**	less spicy	**kam mirch**

...and Read the Menu

baida	egg	**mithai**	sweets
chai	tea	**namak**	salt
dahi	curd/yoghurt	**pani**	water
dudh	milk	**panir**	cheese
lassi	yoghurt drink	**tandur**	oven
biryani	rice cooked with vegetables/meat		
idly	steamed rice cake		
masala dosa	crispy lentil-flour pancake		
pilao	rice cooked with ghi and spices		
uttapam	moist savoury rice-flour pancake		

Breads (Roti)

chapati	flat, unleavened bread
nan	leavened flat bread
paratha	chapati cooked with ghi
puri	deep-fried and puffed-up wheat bread
tanduri roti	similar to nan

Fruit and Vegetables

allu	potato	**gobi**	cauliflower
aum	mango	**kela**	banana
baingain	aubergine	**palak**	spinach
bindi	okra	**mattar**	peas
dal	dried lentils	**santra**	orange

Meat

ghost	lamb
murg	chicken

Fish (Machli)

bummalo	Bombay duck
pomflit	pomfret

HANDY TRAVEL TIPS

An A–Z Summary of Practical Information

A

ACCOMMODATION (See also YOUTH HOSTELS and the list of RECOMMENDED HOTELS starting on page 128)

With pressure on space as acute as it is in Mumbai, demand for hotel beds is considerable. As a consequence, room tariffs here are the highest in India and advance booking at least one month ahead is essential, even at the lower end of the scale.

Hotels are graded into categories by the city's tourist office, ranging from one to five stars. In addition, there are countless ungraded establishments, although some of these may be cramped, poorly furnished and inadequately ventilated, with no en-suite bathrooms or windows, and rooms separated only by a flimsy wood partition. All the unstarred places reviewed in this book offer acceptably clean and honest accommodation for budget travellers.

Mid-range hotels tend to be grouped in quieter parts of town such as Colaba, and have rooms with balconies, tiled bathrooms with showers and Western-style toilets, and cable TVs. Some have air conditioning, which can add 50 percent or more to the tariff (bear in mind that in older hotels the a/c units may be very noisy). The city's four and five star establishments, by contrast, all offer international standards of comfort, including central air conditioning.

As well as a list of regular hotels in the city, the India Government Tourist Office (IGTO) in Churchgate *(see page 126)* also provides addresses for paying guest accommodation – rooms in private family homes. These range from rudimentary budget options to suites in luxury properties, and will, as a rule, provide a more homely atmosphere than is usual for a hotel (though with less privacy).

One factor that might influence where you choose to stay is the proximity of the airports. With the taxi ride into town taking anything up to three or more hours at peak times, visitors in transit tend to opt for somewhere in the north of the city, either in a suburb close to the airports or at nearby Juhu Beach.

AIRPORTS (See also GETTING THERE)

Mumbai is India's principal gateway, with 45 take-offs and landings per hour. In common with many important public facilities in the city, its international wing, Sahar, has been renamed Chhatrapati Shivaji. The domestic terminal is known as Santa Cruz. They lie adjacent to one another, 30km (19 miles) north of Colaba. The taxi ride to either can take as little as one hour, but leave two or three times that length of time during peak periods (8.30–10am and 4–8pm).

For transit between the two airports, free shuttle buses leave every 15 minutes from the main concourses outside Arrivals.

Leaving Chhatrapati Shivaji, you have the option of the cheap Ex-Serviceman's bus, which stops at Santa Cruz en route to several key landmarks in the city, or a taxi from the pre-paid taxi counter in the Arrivals hall. There is no official pre-paid taxi service at Santa Cruz, although some firms may represent themselves as such.

Airport Enquiries. Flight times and general passenger information for both airports is posted at <www.mumbaiairport.com>. For airport information by phone:

International: 2615 6600.
Domestic: 2682 9000.

B

BEGGING

Given the enormous gulf between rich and poor in Mumbai, it should come as no surprise that begging is a way of life for many thousands of homeless, jobless people in the city. As a wealthy foreigner, you'll constantly be approached with requests for money, especially at traffic lights, on trains and walking around the city. Such approaches might be persistent, but they're never aggressive. Whether or not to give, and if so how much, is a matter of personal choice. But to refuse on the grounds that it somehow encourages dependency is nonsense. Very few of the poor people who beg in Mumbai have any means of supporting themselves or their families and will be very grateful for even a small gift – Rs10 will provide a square meal. Many seasoned travellers stock up with small notes and change just for this purpose.

BUDGETING FOR YOUR TRIP

Mumbai is a lot more expensive than the rest of India, although still considerably cheaper than cities in the developed world. Here is a list of approximate costs to help you with your budgeting.

Airport transfer. Taxi from Chhatrapati Shivaji International Airport to the centre of Mumbai Rs350 (£4.50/US$7.65).

Accommodation. Room in mid-range hotel per night (including all taxes) Rs1,300 (£16.50/US$28).

Car hire. Cars with drivers cost Rs1,500–2,000 (£19–26/US$34–45) per day, which should include petrol. The final rate depends on the distance covered.

Meals. Cooked breakfast in your hotel room Rs75 (£1/US$1.65). Light lunch in an inexpensive south Indian café Rs75 (£1/US$1.65). Dinner at an expensive restaurant Rs1,000 (£12.75/US$22).

Sightseeing. Museum admission Rs300 (£3.80/US$6.50). City tour Rs70 (£0.90/US$1.50). Excursion to Elephanta Island Rs100 (£1.30/US$2.20). Flight to Aurangabad (for Ellora and Ajanta caves) Rs2,760 (£35/$60).

C

CAR HIRE

Mumbai's roads are among the most difficult and dangerous in the world, and only the most confident (or foolhardy) of foreign drivers venture on them in a self-drive vehicle. It's far more common to book a car with a driver. This need not be as expensive as you might imagine, and can be easily arranged through the India Government Tourist Office (IGTO) at Churchgate (tel: 2203 3144), or any reputable travel agent.

For city tours, you'll usually pay a flat rate for an eight-hour day covering a maximum of 80km (50 miles), with extra charges for any additional mileage. All rates should be given in writing by the agent or car-hire company before departure. It's also customary to pay for the driver's lunch and a tip at the end of the day. On longer tours, similar rates and restrictions apply; and again, you'll have to cover the driver's meals (though not his lodging as he'll probably sleep in the car).

CLIMATE

Mumbai's position beside the Arabian Sea means its tropical climate sees little seasonal fluctuation in temperature, with thermometers hovering at an average maximum of between 28°C (82°F) and 32°C (90°F) for most of the year. The hottest month is usually May, during the build up to the annual monsoons, which tend to erupt in the first week of June. Heavy downpours are blown in from the west at this time, transforming the city's streets into surging torrents. The heaviest rainfall ever recorded in a city in a single day – 942mm (37.1in) – occurred in Mumbai on 26 July 2005.

In October, the monsoon subsides but leaves in its wake oppressive humidity. Not until the end of November does the air lose most of its moisture. This pleasant winter period, however, only lasts until the end of February. From March onwards, humidity levels and temperatures start to nudge uncomfortably upwards again.

CLOTHING

It never gets cold in Mumbai and you should only need to wrap up if your hotel air-conditioning system gets too fierce. Bring clothes for intense tropical heat and humidity, and make sure they're tough, bearing in mind the rough treatment they'll get at the hands of the city's *dhobi-wallahs* (laundry service, *see page 120*); buttons in particular have a habit of coming back broken from the laundry.

Mumbaikars are conservative dressers by Western standards. Most men wear conventional cotton shirts with collars, smartly creased trousers and shiny shoes. Women will attract a lot less unwanted attention by keeping their arms and legs covered (especially in Muslim districts and crowded markets). This doesn't necessarily apply to smart restaurants, clubs or hotels, however, where dress codes are similar to what you're probably used to at home (albeit with a few more glamorous Indian saris and salwar kameezes). One major difference is that any signs of grubbiness or dishevelment will be considered poor form.

COMPLAINTS

Attitudes to efficiency differ greatly in Mumbai depending on whether a business or service is run by the government (when it'll probably move at a snail's pace, if at all) or a private company (when it'll be done at lightning speed unseen elsewhere in India).

Enterprises of both types routinely offer 'complaint' boxes, ledgers or forms for their customers. In the case of the former, submitting feedback will do little more than assuage your frustration, whereas complaining in the latter instance might well have a tangible result. Bear in mind that – tempting though it might be to stamp your feet and shout when your efforts to, say, book a rail ticket are foiled by an unscheduled tea break – complaints are always more likely to be effective if made politely, to the most senior person available.

CONSULATES (See also CUSTOMS AND ENTRY REQUIREMENTS)

In addition to their embassies or high commissions in the India capital, New Delhi, most foreign countries maintain consulates in Mumbai – useful for replacing lost travel documents.

Australia: 6th Floor, Maker Tower 'E', Cuffe Parade, tel: 2218 1071. Open 9am–5pm.

Canada: 41/42 Maker Chambers VI, Nariman Point, tel: 2287 6027. Open 9am–5.30pm.

Republic of Ireland: Royal Bombay Yacht Club Chambers, Apollo Bunder, tel: 2202 4607. Open 9.30am–1pm.

Singapore: 10th Floor, Maker Chamber IV, 222 Jamnal Bajaj Marg, Nariman Point, tel: 2204 3205. Open 9am–noon.
South Africa: Gandhi Mansion, 20 Altamount Road, tel: 2389 3725. Open 9am–noon.
UK: 2nd Floor, Maker Chamber IV, Nariman Point, tel: 2283 0517. Open 8am–11.30am.
US: Lincoln House, 78 Bhulabhai Desai Road, tel: 2363 3611. Open 8.30am–11am.

CRIME AND SAFETY (See also EMERGENCIES)

Mumbai is, on the whole, a safe and secure city for visitors; very few travellers ever experience problems more serious than being overcharged by a cabbie or porter. That said, a few common-sense precautions should be observed. Pickpocketing is rife in railway stations and on Mumbai's more crowded streets. It's better not to carry around more cash than you need, and to keep credit cards, travel documents and other valuables under lock and key back at your hotel (most hotels have safe-deposit facilities). Before leaving home, always make a photocopy of your passport, including its identification pages, and all visas, in case it is lost or stolen.

In the event of any crime, particularly one for which you might later wish to file an insurance claim, go immediately to the nearest police station (your hotel will know where it is) and lodge a 'complaint' or 'incident report'. Make sure it's signed, dated and stamped, and copy the document at the first opportunity.

As with anywhere else in the world, the risk of sexual violence is a fact of life women should bear in mind when venturing out at night, or alone in taxis. Exercise the same caution as you would at home.

CUSTOMS AND ENTRY REQUIREMENTS

Visitors of all nationalities – except Nepalis and Bhutanis – need a visa to enter India. Standard multiple-entry tourist visas are valid for six months and cost £30/US$60. They're available by post from any Indian embassy, high commission or consulate.

Indian embassies and high commissions abroad:

Australia High Commission: 3–5 Moonah Place, Yarralumla, Canberra, ACT 2600, tel: 02-6273 3999, <www.highcommissionofindiaaustralia.org>.

Canada High Commission: 10 Springfield Road, Ottawa, Ontario K1M 1C9, tel: 613-744 3751, <www.hciottawa.ca>.

New Zealand High Commission: 180 Molesworth Street (P.O. Box 4005), Wellington, tel: 04-473 6390, <www.hicomind.org.nz>.

Singapore Embassy: India House, 31 Grange Road (P.O. Box 9123), Singapore, tel: 0923-737 6777, <www.embassyofindia.com>.

UK High Commission: India House, Aldwych, London WC2B 4NA, tel: 020 7836 8484, <www.hcilondon.org>.

US Embassy of India (Consular Services): 2107 Massachusetts Avenue NW, Washington DC 20008, tel: 202-939 7000.

Duty-free allowance. Foreign tourists, other than those from neighbouring states, are permitted to import a maximum of 200 cigarettes or 50 cigars or 250g of tobacco, and 1 litre of wine or spirits.

Currency. There is no upper limit on the amount of foreign currency visitors are permitted to bring to India, but you're not permitted to take any rupees out of the country without clearance – it is more trouble than it's worth unless you're in business and can employ someone to arrange the necessary paperwork on your behalf.

E

ELECTRICITY

India operates on 220V 50Hz AC, with two or three round-pin plugs. Visitors from the UK, Ireland and Australia will get by with an adapter; US and Canadian appliances, however, might also need a transformer.

Electricity supplies are generally reliable in Mumbai, except during the monsoons when power cuts are frequent. Power surges, on the other hand, are common, so before plugging in any sensitive electrical equipment such as a laptop computer you should consider investing in a current stabiliser (or UPS, as they're known).

Indian batteries tend to run out a lot more quickly than those you're probably used to, so bring a supply from home.

EMERGENCIES

Ambulance	102
Fire	101
Police	100

G

GAY AND LESBIAN TRAVELLERS

Mumbai is far and away India's most 'out' city, though attitudes remain conservative by Western standards. In India, for example, 'carnal intercourse against the laws of nature' (i.e. anal sex) carries a 10-year prison sentence (the law is rarely enforced, but often used by policemen to lever bribes).

Published in Mumbai, *Bombay Dost* is a magazine that supports gay, lesbian, bisexual and transgender communities throughout the country and its listings pages are a useful resource for nightlife. Its website (<www.bombaydost.com>) is a mine of information. Best known of all the city's gay and lesbian hangouts, though a bit sleazy, is the Voodoo Pub, 2–5 Kamal Mansion, Arthur Bunder Road, Colaba.

The organisation Gaybombay arranges parties twice each month, as well as monthly mini film festivals. For more on gay life in Mumbai, check out <www.gaybombay.org>. Support and contacts for lesbians are available through the group Humjinsi, India Centre For Human Rights and Law, 4th Floor, CVOD Jain School, 84 Samuel Street (Pala Galli), Dongri (tel: 2343 9651).

GETTING THERE (See also AIRPORTS)

Mumbai is the easiest city in India to reach from abroad, with a wider choice of air connections than anywhere else in the country. Coming from other Indian cities, you have a correspondingly broad array of overland transport options.

By air (international). Mumbai's Chhatrapati Shivaji Airport is the busiest in India, hosting upwards of 45 landings and departures daily. All the main carriers flying through Asia stop over here. The best way of picking through the many and convoluted route options that'll be open to you from wherever you're travelling is to let a travel agent do it on your behalf.

With a little more time and patience, it's also possible to track down discounted tickets yourself via the internet, through online agents such as <www.expedia.com>, <www.cheapflights.com> and <www.flights4less.co.uk>. The airlines themselves also sell tickets via their websites, though you might only be offered published fares.

Ticket prices remain fairly constant year round, rising only a little over major holidays such as Diwali and Christmas.

By air (domestic). Scheduled flights leave Mumbai's Santa Cruz domestic airport for more than 24 different Indian destinations. The three main carriers are Indian Airlines <www.indian-airlines.nic.in>, Jet Airways <www.jetairways.com> and Air Sahara <www.airsahara.net>. Tickets may be purchased direct through the airlines' offices or websites, or through a travel agent; foreigners and non-resident Indians (NRIs) are obliged to pay a higher fare, quoted in US dollars.

In addition, several low-cost alternatives have sprung up recently offering much cheaper tickets to Mumbai from a range of major Indian cities. These include Air Deccan <www.airdeccan.net>, Kingfisher Airlines <www.flykingfisher.com> and Spicejet <www.spicejet.com>. Foreigners and NRIs pay the same as resident Indian passport holders, and bookings have to be made either online or through the airlines' call centres.

By train. Three different train lines – the Central Railway, the Western Railway and Konkan Railway – converge on Mumbai. Booking tickets on them is a lot easier than it used to be before the advent of computers, but it's still a hit-and-miss affair. Demand nearly always outstrips supply and seats have to be reserved weeks, or months, in advance on popular routes such as those to Mumbai.

Purchasing tickets is marginally easier for foreigners and NRIs than for resident Indians. At stations in major Indian cities, tourists can access a special quota to release seats on heavily booked trains. If this still doesn't work, there's always the option of a Tatkal ticket. This is a new premium service whereby the passenger is charged a supplement of Rs150 over the published fare to obtain tickets from a separate quota. The catch is you have to pay the entire cost of the journey from the originating to terminating station, which is fine if you got on where the train started, but not so great if you pick up the Calcutta–Mumbai express somewhere in central India.

By bus. A vast fleet of buses descends on Mumbai from all over southern and western India each morning, having rattled over bumpy, unlit roads through the night. They range from ultra-basic, beaten-up government buses to 'de-luxe' coaches with hydraulic suspension, push-back seats, couchettes and relentless *'filmi'* videos. The one thing they all have in common, however, is that compared with any other form of transport they offer a much more gruelling, and dangerous, way to travel. Unless you're desperate to save money, go by train or plane.

GUIDES AND TOURS

Official guides can be hired through the India Government Tourist Office (IGTO) at Churchgate; they'll show you around any of the sights covered in this book, and will create a tailor-made itinerary.

A less expensive option are the city tours on open-topped buses laid on by the Maharashtra Tourism Development Corporation or MTDC (Tues–Sun 2–6pm; admission charges cost extra), which pack

Mumbai's main points of interest into a half day. Tickets can be purchased from their office on Madam Cama Road – the departure point.

H

HEALTH AND MEDICAL CARE

Given the potential health risks of travelling to India, it's essential to seek medical advice before leaving home. No vaccinations are mandatory, but some – including cholera, typhoid, hepatitis and tetanus – may be strongly recommended. In addition, some form of protection against malaria is essential, particularly during and immediately after the monsoons, when infection rates soar.

The most common ailment suffered by travellers to the city, however, is an upset stomach caused by contaminated food, which can

---

Golden Rules for Staying Healthy in Mumbai

Most health troubles that afflict travellers in Mumbai can be easily avoided by observing some simple dos and don'ts:

- Drink plenty of fluids at all times.
- Never get bitten by mosquitos; smother any exposed skin in repellent in the evenings and wear long sleeves and trousers.
- Get lots of sleep (ear plugs may prove useful).
- Stay away from food that looks like it's been reheated or left in the open; and avoid empty restaurants. Only eat meat in busy restaurants with a fast turnover.
- Don't drink the tap water, not even to brush your teeth; stick to the bottled variety, soft drinks, tea or coffee (or minimise plastic pollution by bringing water purification tablets).
- Go easy on alcohol: most Indian beers and spirits are laced with nasty preservatives that can play havoc with your stomach.

result in diarrhoea. The best treatment for this is to lay off meals for 24 hours, and to drink plenty of fluids, ideally laced with rehydration salts (available through any pharmacy). Should you pass blood or mucus, or if the diarrhoea persists for more than three or four days and is accompanied by a fever, contact a doctor. This can be most easily done through your hotel, guesthouse or local hosts.

If you should need to visit a hospital for any reason, the best one in the city centre is the Bombay Hospital, <www.bombayhospital. com>, at New Marine Lines, just north of the India Government Tourist Office in Churchgate.

HOLIDAYS

The following are official public holidays in Mumbai. Precise dates of most religious festivals change according to lunar and astrological calendars of their respective faith communities; secular ones remain the same from year to year.

January–February	Bakri-Id (Id-Uz-Zua)
26 January	Republic Day
February–March	Mahashivratri
March–April	Good Friday
	Holi (Second Day)
	Gudi Padwa
14 April	Dr Babasaheb Ambedkar Jayanti
April	Ram Navami
April–May	Mahavir Jayanti
May–June	Buddha Purnima
15 August	Independence Day
August–September	Parsi New Year Day (Shahenshahi)
	Ganesh Chaturthi
October	Dasara
	Ramzan Id (Id-Ul-Fitar)

2 October	Mahatma Gandhi's Birthday
October–November	Diwali Amavasya (Laxmi Pujan)
November	Guru Nanak Jayanti
25 December	Christmas Day

L

LANGUAGE

English is the first language of most educated Mumbaikars, albeit a heavily accented version liberally laced with words in Hindi, India's official lingua franca. The only situations where you're ever likely to need basic Hindi is when shopping in the central bazaar areas. If you venture outside south Mumbai, taxi drivers might also only have a few words of English. Maharashtra's state language is Marathi.

Hello/Goodbye	**namaste**
Yes	**ha**
No	**naihee**
How much?	**kitna paisa?**
How far is the Jama Masjid?	**Jama Masijd kitna dur hai?**
Thank you	**dhaniywad** (Hindu)/
	shukriya (Muslim)
I don't understand	**naihee samajtai hai**
Do you speak English?	**English bulta?**
My name is (Sunil)	**Meera naam (Sunil) hai**
one	**ek**
two	**doh**
three	**teen**
four	**char**
five	**panch**
six	**che**
seven	**saarth**
eight	**aarth**

nine	**nau**
ten	**das**
twenty	**bis**
thirty	**tis**
forty	**chalis**
fifty	**pachis**
one hundred	**so**
two hundred	**do so**
one thousand	**ek hazaa**

As befits a country of exceedingly large numbers, India has its own term to describe one hundred thousand – a 'lakh'. One hundred million is a 'crore'.

LAUNDRY SERVICES

Virtually all hotels in Mumbai offer laundry *(dhobi)* services, although if you're staying in an expensive place you could save hundreds of rupees by taking your wash to a high-street 'dry cleaners' instead. "Dry', however, is something of a misnomer, as what actually happens is that your clothes are taken to the municipal *dhobi* ghats at Mahalakshmi, or a nearby equivalent, soaked in soapy water by *dhobi-wallahs* and pounded with wooden bats until clean.

LEFT LUGGAGE

Although many left luggage facilities close periodically in response to security alerts, there should in principal be places where you can leave your bags outside the airport terminals, and at major train stations (where they're known as 'cloakrooms'). The minimum charge covers 24 hours or any part thereof, and each article of luggage must be locked, even rucksacks. In addition, your hotel may agree to look after any bags you might wish to leave with them while away from the city for short periods; again, ensure they are all locked and clearly labelled with your name and address.

M

MAPS

The maps featured inside the covers of this book should suffice for the purposes of sightseeing, but if you'd like a more detailed version, hunt out Eicher's *City Map: Mumbai*, a 185-page A–Z featuring every street and landmark, plus a comprehensive index. It's available in most good book shops.

Free fold-up maps of Mumbai and its suburbs are handed out by the tourist office in Churchgate *(see page 126)*.

MEDIA

India's two main daily broadsheets – *The Times of India* and *Indian Express* – both publish local editions with specific coverage of Mumbai, from politics to sport and the arts. You'll find them at every news vendor's stand, along with a huge range of glossies. For weekly news roundups, political features and coverage of India-wide current affairs, the *Time*-style magazines *India Today*, *Outlook* and *Frontline* are worth a browse. Local editions of the dailies all feature 'What's On' sections, as well as useful timetable details for flights and trains, and tide times (handy if you're heading for Haji Ali's tomb). But for in-depth previews and listings of arts and cultural events, the indispensable source is *Time Out: Mumbai*.

Bollywood gossip fills magazines such as *Cine Blitz*, *Film Fare* and *Stardust*, all of which make lurid, and sometimes hilarious, reading. The same can't be said of India's women's magazines, *Elle* and *Cosmopolitan*, which are more conservative than their Western counterparts, focusing on fashion and lifestyle for India's elite.

MONEY

India's currency is the rupee (Rs), divided into 100 paise. Coins come in units of 5, 10, 25 and 50 paise, and 1, 2 and 5 rupees. Bank notes exist in denominations of Rs5, 10, 20, 50, 100 and 500. It can sometimes be difficult to distinguish between the Rs100 and Rs500 notes, especially to begin with, or in dim light.

There exists throughout India a chronic shortage of small notes. Taxi drivers and rickshaw-*wallahs* in particular will rarely admit to having any, forcing you to part with yours or engage in a bluff of your own. When exchanging currency, therefore, it's a good idea to request part of the sum to be in small denominations.

Excessive wear and tear on the few small notes that are in circulation has reduced most of them to a dreadful state. This wouldn't be such a problem if Indians weren't so picky about the condition of money paid to them, but the tiniest of rips will be grounds enough to refuse a note – the source of another national pastime similar to holding on to one's change is trying to palm off the spoiled notes that someone else has palmed off on you. It's a game Mumbai's taxi drivers and street vendors are well practised at, so expect grubby, holed and torn Rs5 notes to build up after a time. However, you can exchange the notes for new ones at a bank; better still, you could give them to someone on the street who looks like they might need them more than you (*see* BEGGING).

Banks and exchange. Foreign currency and travellers cheques may be exchanged at most banks during working hours (Mon–Fri 10am–5pm, Sat 10am–noon). You'll be charged a percentage commission or flat fee for the service, but the main disadvantage with drawing money this way are the often long waits involved for the paperwork to inch its way through the ranks of sleepy clerks and tellers.

If you've brought American Express or Thomas Cook travellers cheques, it's worth going out of your way to change them free of commission at dedicated offices of American Express on Shivaji Marg, around the corner from the Regal cinema in Colaba (open Mon–Fri 9.30am–5.30pm, Sat 9.30am–2pm, tel: 2204 8291 or 989-260 0800) or Thomas Cook, Dr D.N. Marg, Fort (open Mon–Sat 9.30am–7pm, tel: 2204 8556).

Credit and debit cards. The major plastic payment cards are accepted at most upscale shops, hotels and restaurants in Mumbai, but if you're in any doubt check first. Also, it's wise to ensure that if the transaction is made using an old-fashioned paper docket rather than chip-and-pin handset, you don't let your card out of your sight.

Cash dispensers, or ATMs, are attached to all major banks these days (usually in air-conditioned annexes guarded by armed doormen), and these offer a fast and convenient way to withdraw money. In terms of cost, exchanging cash at an ATM may even work out cheaper than travellers' cheques: the exchange rates are usually better and the transaction charges lower (though the percentage of commission should be checked with your bank before leaving home).

The main disadvantage of relying on a credit or debit card as your main source of currency is that you'll be in a sticky situation should you lose it, or if it's swallowed by the ATM (Indian banks are obliged to return any withheld cards to their originating branch, even if it's abroad). Always carry some kind of back up, and bring some emergency hard currency or travellers' cheques too, along with the telephone number of your bank at home should you need to contact it urgently.

OPENING HOURS

Mumbai might be the City That Never Sleeps, but as a consequence it makes a sluggish start to the day. Even breakfast places tend not to open until 9am or later. Banks start at 10am and close at 2.30pm, Mon–Fri, or at 12.30pm on Saturdays. Shops generally open at 10am and close and 7pm, Mon–Sat.

As for government offices, timings vary between places, but as a rule of thumb most work Mon–Fri 10am–6pm. Opening hours of attractions and sights are given in the *Where to Go* section of this guide.

P

POLICE (See also EMERGENCIES)

Indian police have earned a reputation for being incorrigibly corrupt, and Mumbai's cops are no exception. As a foreigner, any dealings with the police – such as reporting thefts of valuables or a passport – are likely to involve requests for a small bribe – Rs100 rupees should suffice to oil the wheels. Should you be arrested for any reason, contact your consulate at the first opportunity.

POST OFFICES

Mumbai's venerable old General Post Office on Nagar Chowk is open daily Mon–Sat 9am–8pm and Sun 10am–5pm. Stamps can be bought from the counters inside, but you'll have to affix them with glue (pots of revolting flour-based gloop are provided). Airmail letters cost Rs11, or Rs6.50 for an aerogram and Rs6 for a postcard.

Parcels have to be wrapped in cotton, stitched and sealed in wax – a row of *parcel-wallahs* seated outside the GPO will do this for you. Unless you don't mind waiting weeks or months for your package to arrive, it's worth sending it via Speed Post. This premium service costs Rs20–60 for up to 500g inland, or Rs425–625 (up to 500g and Rs75–100 for every 250g thereafter) to foreign countries.

PUBLIC TRANSPORT

Millions of Mumbaikars will be on the move at any given moment and if you're planning to explore the city in any depth it pays to pick your time and mode of transport carefully.

Taxis. Mumbai's black-and-yellow cabs, which queue outside major hotels and can be flagged down on the road at any time of the day or night, are by far the most convenient way to nip around town. They're all metered and the driver will have a 'tariff' card to convert the fare shown to the actual fare; you'll also have to pay extra for luggage. At busy times, however, many cabbies refuse to use their meters, in which case you'll have to haggle a fare in advance.

Trains. Suburban trains to and from Mumbai's main terminus stations, Churchgate and CST (VT) transport an army of commuters daily. They get horrendously cramped, with passengers literally dangling out of the doors. They are best avoided. The one exception is to Kanheri and Vasai Road (for Bassein Fort), which can be done in relative comfort, and cheaply, provided you avoid rush hours.

Buses. Run by the Brihanmumbai Electric Supply and Transport Company (BEST for short), Mumbai's red buses are just as packed as the trains. Moreover, finding out which ones go where can prove a major research project, while to make matters still more confusing for foreigners, their route numbers and destinations are often displayed in Marathi. All in all, you're better off jumping in a cab.

R

RELIGION

Nearly 70 percent of Mumbai's population are Hindus. Muslims make up the largest minority community, at 17 percent, with Christians and Buddhists at 4 percent each. The city also hosts smaller minorities of Jains, Parsis, Sikhs and Jews.

T

TELEPHONE

Mumbai's STD code is 022 and the country code is +91. When calling any number in Mumbai from outside India, say the UK, drop the initial 0 from the city code and dial 00 91 22, then the eight digits.

Privately run telephone booths pop up on every other corner in Mumbai. Designated by yellow STD/ISD (Standard Trunk Dialling/

International Subscriber Dialling) signboards, they're efficient and easy to use. As soon as you're connected, an electronic meter kicks in, showing you the duration and cost of the call; you pay at the end. Charges for trunk and international calls are very expensive, though fall considerably after 8pm.

Mobiles. Charges for mobile calls are far lower in India than most Western countries, which is why many visitors who plan to spend much time in the city sign up with a local network, such as Airtel, BPL or Idea. To do this, you must buy a SIM card from a mobile phone shop; the dealer will help install it and get you connected.

TIME DIFFERENCE

Indian Standard Time is GMT plus 5½ hours, winter and summer.

TIPPING

Tipping is commonplace in hotels: a Rs10 or Rs20 note should be adequate for porters and room service (though in four- and five-star hotels, staff often expect Rs50). For good service in a restaurant or from a taxi driver, you might wish to tip 10 or 15 percent of your bill

TOILETS

There are very few public toilets in Mumbai, and those that exist are generally in a poor state. If you need to use the loo, look for a smart restaurant or café: the washrooms off the lobby of the Taj Mahal Palace and Tower, to the left of the main reception desk, are some of the most sumptuous in India, though you'll have to be smartly dressed and pretend you're using the hotel's other facilities to gain entry.

TOURIST INFORMATION

Mumbai's most helpful tourist office is the government-run IGTO, <www.india-tourism.org>, by the east exit of Churchgate Station, at 123 Madam Karve Road (open Mon–Fri 8.30am–6pm, Sun 8.30am–2pm, tel: 2203 3144). Both airports have 24-hour information desks.

W

WEBSITES AND INTERNET CAFES

Most starred hotels offer internet access to guests. The British Council Library, on the first floor of A-Wing, Mittal Tower, Barrister Rajni Patel Marg, Nariman Point (open Tues–Sat 10am–5.45pm), has a fast ADSL connection. Failing these options, you'll have to resort to one of the cramped internet cafés off SBS Marg (Colaba's main street). Many other places providing internet access have also opened up around Churchgate and Fort – just look out for their signboards.

The following websites provide useful information on Mumbai: <www.mumbainet.com>, <www.mumbaizone.com>, <www.india express.com/news/regional/maharashtra/bombay>, <www.timesof india.com>, <www.filmfare.com>,<www.bollywoodworld.com>, <www.mumbai-central.com>, <http://web.mid-day.com>.

WEIGHTS AND MEASURES

All but the most remote parts of India have embraced the metric system. Distances are measured in metres and kilometres. Weights are given in grammes and kilograms ('kg'). Two notable exceptions are jewellery and precious metals, which are weighed in old-style *tolas* – one tola being the weight of a British East India Company rupee: 11.66 grams.

Y

YOUTH HOSTELS

The YWCA, located on Madam Cama Road, and the Salvation Army's Red Shield House, are both open to non-members (you pay for membership in the room tariff) and offer some of the best-value accommodation in the city. The YWCA is more like a hotel and not as cheap as the latter. *(See RECOMMENDED HOTELS on pages 130 and 131.)*

Recommended Hotels

Tariffs do not fluctuate according to the season, but are subject to government 'luxury' taxes, levied at the rate of 4 percent on rooms costing Rs200–1,199, or at 10 percent if your room costs more than Rs1,200 per night; make sure when you book that these have been included in the quoted rate or you could get a shock when you come to pay. Check-out times vary, but are often earlier than you might expect; some, especially in hotels close to the airports, are 24-hours from check-in time.

Reservations may be made by telephone, post or email, although it's customary to request a deposit or credit card number as security. Note that at the top end of the scale, hotels tend to offer their best rates online rather than over the phone.

When calling any number in Mumbai from outside India, drop the initial 0 from Mumbai's STD code (022): dial 00 91 22 and then the eight remaining digits.

$$$$$	Over Rs3,000
$$$$	Rs2,000–3,000
$$$	Rs1,000–2,000
$$	Rs500–1,000
$	Below Rs500

COLABA

Ascot $$$$ *38 Garden Road, tel: 2284 0020 or 2287 2105, <www.ascothotel.com>.* Spruce, stylish three-star hotel sporting a trendy new look, though it's been here for years. Excellent value in its bracket, with most of the mod cons you'd expect (including in-room internet access and safe deposits), though no pool.

Bentley's $$$ *17 Oliver Road, tel: 2284 1474, <www.bentleys hotel.com>.* Old-fashioned, homely hotel occupying no less than four of Colaba's atmospheric colonial-era tenements. Most of the rooms have balconies and good-sized windows; the pricier ones are well worth the extra, with lots of space and, in some cases, period furniture. The main (reception) block has a leafy garden at the back of it.

Causeway $$$ *43/45 Mathurades Estate, SBS Marg, tel: 2281 7777, <www.hotelcauseway.com>.* A small, popular hotel on Colaba's main street. Its 25 rooms all have air conditioning, contemporary decor and en-suite bathrooms. Avoid those on the front of the building, which are noisier (despite the soundproofing). Online booking available.

Fariyas $$$$$ *25 Arthur Road, tel: 2204 2911, <www.fariyas. com>.* On the quiet side of Colaba, this pint-sized four-star hotel is popular with business clients, though it lacks the cachet of the Taj. The pool is really small. Harbour views cost extra.

Godwin $$$$ *Jasmine Building, 41 Garden Road, tel: 2287 2050, email: <hotelgodwin@mail.com>.* The rooms on the upper storeys of this compact three-star benefit from panoramic views over south Mumbai's convoluted skyline. All have good-sized bathrooms, fridges and TVs; there's a bar-restaurant on the ground floor. Airport transfer available on request.

Gorden House $$$$$ *5 Battery Street, Apollo Bunder, tel: 2287 1122, <www.ghhotel.com>.* Hip 'boutique' hotel, with variously themed rooms and suites (eg 'Scandinavian', 'American Country', etc). It's bright, stylish, modern and centrally air conditioned, with CD players and cable TVs in every room, and a popular 'wok' restaurant at street level.

Harbour View $$$$ *Kerawalla Chambers, 25 PJ Ramchandani Marg, tel: 2284 1197, <www.viewhotelsindia.com>.* At an unbeatable location on Apollo Bunder, the hotel has enormous rooms with some wonderful views, although you certainly have to pay a premium for such a room with a view. This establishment is at its best in the rooftop restaurant, which ranks among the most relaxing places to hang out in the city.

Lawrence $ *3rd Floor, 33 Sri Sai Baba Marg (Rope Walk Lane), off K. Dubash Marg, tel: 2284 3618 or 5633 6107*. Very basic budget hotel, run by a Goan family in the heart of Kala Ghoda. Its rooms, though plain, are clean and well aired, and the rates unbeatable – hence the waiting list (book at least a month in advance). The entrance is up the lane behind TGI's.

Moti International $$ *10 Best Marg, tel: 2202 1654 or 2202 5714, email: <hotelmotiinternational@yahoo.com.in>*. Small, friendly budget hotel, with a range of inexpensive rooms (from simple bathroom-less doubles to large air-conditioned suites) in a colonial-era building. They're cool, quiet and clean (if showing signs of age) and the management is welcoming.

Red Shield $ *Red Shield House, 30 Mereweather Road, near the Taj, tel: 2284 1824*. Run by the Salvation Army, this well-managed hostel has cheap dorm beds or large en-suite doubles – both at bargain rates that include full board. Amazing value for money for the area, though some find the atmosphere a bit institutional.

Regent $$$$ *8 Best Road, tel: 2287 1854, email: <hotelregent@vsnl.com>*. Efficient, modern place whose fully en-suite, air-conditioned rooms are on the small side, but perfectly comfortable, with soundproofed windows.

Sea Palace $$$$ *Kerawalla Chambers, 26 PJ Ramchandani Marg, tel: 2284 1828, <www.seapalacehotel.com>*. Recently refurbished hotel in a rather grand building facing the seafront where the P&O steamers used to tie up. The rooms are equipped with internet connections, fridges and cable TVs as standard; there's a multi-cuisine restaurant.

Sea Shore $$ *4th Floor, 1–49 Kamal Mansion, Arthur Bunder Road, tel: 2287 4237*. The most dependable and secure of the low-budget hotels in Colaba. Only half of its rooms have windows and none are en suite, but everything is kept spic-and-span and the management are unfailingly courteous. Handy safe-deposit and left-luggage facilities are also available.

Shelley's $$$$ *30 PJ Ramchandani Marg, tel: 2284 0229, <www.shellyshotel.com>.* Faded but very appealing old hotel that's been in business since British times and altered little since (though it was refurbished quite recently). The rooms have retained some period charm. Go for one of the sea-facing options, which have small balconies.

Taj Mahal Palace & Tower $$$$$ *PJ Ramchandani Marg, tel: 5665 3366, <www.tajhotels.com>.* India's most famous hotel, and the flagship five-star of the Taj Group luxury chain, is every bit as grand as you'd expect. Its most elegant rooms are those in the seven-storey old wing, though the views are better from the top of the rather ugly Moorish Tower next door. Facilities include several superb restaurants, a shopping mall, huge outdoor pool, gym, steam room and nightclub.

Taj President $$$$$ *90 Cuffe Parade, tel: 5665 0808, <www.tajhotels.com>.* Taj Group's other five-star in south Mumbai occupies an 18-floor skyscraper, 10 minutes by taxi from the Gateway of India. Although lacking the grandeur of the Taj Mahal Palace, it's considerably less expensive and it's popular with international business clients. Off the lobby is a comfy bar and fabulous Mangalorean restaurant, the Konkan Café *(see page 138)*, as well as an outdoor pool with an adjacent steam room and gym.

YWCA $$$–$$$$ *18 Madam Cama Road, tel: 2202 5053, <www.ywcaic.info>.* Both men and women are welcome to stay at this immaculate 'Y' near the museum, which has cheap doubles and family rooms as well as dorm beds. It's more formal and better furnished (though pricier) than the Red Shield *(see opposite)*. Rates cover obligatory club membership and half board.

CHURCHGATE, FORT & MARINE DRIVE

Ambassador $$$$$ *VN Road, tel: 2204 1131, <www.ambassadorindia.com>.* Grand four-star which, though in need of refurbishment, is in a great location just off Marine Drive, and has superb views over the whole city from its revolving restaurant.

Bentley $$ *3rd Floor, Krishna Mahal, Marine Drive, tel: 2281 5244.* Modest, quiet guesthouse, located a stone's throw away from Wankhede Stadium on the seafront. Its rooms share bathrooms, but are cool, marble-lined and clean, and very good value for the area. Rates include 'toast-butter-tea' breakfast.

Chateau Windsor $$$$ *5th Floor, 86 VN Road, tel: 2204 4455, <www.chateauwindsor.com>.* Popular mid-range hotel, locked in a 1950s' time warp but impeccably clean and tidy. The rooms are priced according to levels of comfort rather than the views, so if you would like a view, ask for one that's facing the street (as these have small balconies).

Intercontinental $$$$$ *135 Marine Drive, tel: 3987 9999, <www.intercontinental.com>.* Ultra-slick 'boutique' hotel fitted out with designer furniture, in-room broadband, plasma-screen TVs and other up-to-the-minute gadgets. The views over Back Bay from its sea-facing suites are superb; plus there's a fashionable terrace restaurant on the roof, and a very hip vodka bar on the ground floor.

Marine Plaza $$$$$ *29 Marine Drive, tel: 2285 1212, <www.sarovarparkplaza.com>.* Overlooking the bay, this retro-Art Deco five-star is famous for its glass-bottomed rooftop pool. With luxurious rooms and all the usual facilities, it's a good choice if you want the comfort but find larger five stars too impersonal.

New Bengal $–$$$ *Dr DN Marg, tel: 2340 1951, <www.hotel newbengal.com>.* A good economic option if you want to be in the thick of things, close to Crawford Market and central Mumbai, but only a short taxi ride from Colaba. Aimed at visiting businessmen on low budgets, the accommodation is decidedly no frills, ranging from low-ceilinged, airless dorms to more spacious doubles with air conditioning. This is not somewhere that you'd want to spend more than a night or two, but it's clean and safe.

Oberoi/Oberoi Towers $$$$$ *Nariman Point, tel: 2232 5757, <www.oberoihotels.com>.* This pair of ultra-luxurious five-star hotels is where Bill Clinton stayed on his state visit to Mumbai in

2000, and it remains one of the country's top hotels. The complex is divided into two separate sister concerns: the Oberoi is marginally classier, but the views over Back Bay are more impressive from the top of the Oberoi Tower.

Residency $$$ *26 Rustom Sidhwa Marg, tel: 5667 0555, <www.residencyhotel.com>*. Very comfortable, recently refurbished two-star, occupying a converted fire station in the heart of the business district. The decor is contemporary, dominated by mellow browns and creams, and the facilities bang up to date, though they've tried to preserve some of the building's heritage feel. Great value at this price, and in a prime spot in the thick of Fort.

Sea Green South $$$$ *145A Marine Drive, tel: 5633 6535, <www.seagreensouth.com>*. The best thing about this mid-range hotel, housed in one of the seafront's Art Deco apartment blocks, is its location looking across the bay to Malabar Hill. The rooms are air-conditioned and comfortable, though showing signs of wear.

The Shalimar $$$$$ *August Kranti Marg, tel: 5664 1000, <www.theshalimarhotel.com>*. Housed in a modern eight-storey tower block amid the bright lights of Kemp's Corner, just north of Chowpatty Beach, this is a slicker-than-average four-star. The decor is minimalist and contemporary, with warm colours and carpets, and the rooms are spacious for the price.

NEAR CST (VT) RAILWAY STATION

City Palace $$$ *121 City Terrace, tel: 2261 5515, email: <hotel citypalace@vsnl.net>*. Slap opposite CST (VT) railway station, and clean enough, though its cheaper rooms lack windows. Air conditioning available. Convenient if you're having to catch an early-morning train.

Grand $$$$–$$$$$ *17 Shri SR Marg, Ballard Estate, tel: 5658 0500, fax: 5658 0501, <www.grandhotelbombay.com>*. This is a lovely old colonial-style hotel which is located near the docks. It is one of the few places in its class which has an authentic pre-

Independence atmosphere about it – however, it is very expensive and decidedly overpriced.

Manama $$ *221–225 P. D'Mello Road, tel: 2261 3412*. No-frills budget place a short walk from CST (its main asset). Nothing to write home about, but comfy and clean enough for a night, with windows, freshly laundered towels and starched white sheets. Most of the guests are train travellers in transit.

NEAR THE AIRPORT

Aircraft International $$ *179 Dayaldas Road, tel: 2612 1419*. Accommodation around the airport at the budget end of the scale is generally ropey, with cramped, windowless, grubby rooms the norm. This place, though, is well maintained and good value, offering larger than average clean rooms (most with at least one window) at affordable rates. It's only five minutes' walk from the nearest suburban railway station, and a quick taxi ride from the airports.

Bawa International $$$$$ *Vile Parle (East), tel: 2611 3636, <www.bawahotels.com>*. This is a bright, modern transit hotel located next to the domestic airport, Santa Cruz. Courtesy buses to and from the airport are available.

The Emerald $$$$$ *Juhu Tara Road, Juhu, tel: 2661 1150, <www.theemerald.com>*. This Best Western establishment positioned behind Juhu Beach offers a wide range of luxury accommodation, from standard business rooms and suites to one-, two- and three-bedroom apartments with fully equipped kitchenettes. Convenient for the airport, which is just 7km (4 miles) to the east.

Holiday Inn $$$$$ *Balraj Sahani Marg, Juhu, tel: 2693 4444, <www.holidayinnbombay.com>*. A typical Holiday Inn, just as you would expect to find anywhere else in the world, with a pool and international-style restaurants and bars. However, it overlooks the very Indian Juhu Beach, so when you wake up and wonder which country you're in, you can look out of the window. It's an easy half-hour's drive from the airport.

ISKCON $$$ *Juhu Church Road, tel: 2620 6860, <www.iskcon mumbai.com>.* One of the city's more eccentric hotels, run by the International Society for Krishna Consciousness. The tower block building and furnishings are an elaborate fusion of mock-Moghul, Gujarati and Western styles, and the rooms are huge for the price, though certain restrictions apply (you're not allowed to consume alcohol, meat or caffeine on the premises). The hotel's restaurant offers sumptuous vegetarian buffets as an alternative. Book between 10am and 5pm only.

Lotus Suites $$$$$ *Andheri Kurla Road, International Airport Zone, Andheri (East), tel: 2827 0707, <www.lotussuites.com>.* This determinedly 'green' hotel bills itself as an 'Eco Five-Star at Three-Star prices'. A convenient, comfortable option close to the international airport.

Midland $$$$ *Jawaharlal Nehru Road, Santa Cruz (East), tel: 2611 0413, <www.hotelmidland.com>.* This hotel numbers among the few dependable two-stars that are within striking distance of the two airports. Room rates include a courtesy bus to and from the airports and breakfast.

Orchid $$$$$ *70-C Nehru Road, Vile Parle (East), tel: 2616 4040, <www.orchidhotel.com>.* Ground-breaking 'Eco Five Star' hotel whose every feature, from the swimming pool right down to the laundry service and coathangers, has been designed to minimise environmental impact.

Samrat $$$ *3rd Road, Khar West, near Khar railway station, tel: 2648 5441, <www.hotelsinghs.com>.* Rudimentary economy hotel in a lower-middle-class suburb that serves as a handy budget option if you're passing through Mumbai.

Sea Princess $$$$$ *Juhu Tara Road, Juhu, tel: 2661 1111, <www.seaprincess.com>.* Most appealing among the rank of swish five-star hotels backing on to Juhu Beach, with pleasantly furnished rooms and a small swimming pool. Again, only a 30-minute drive from the airport.

Recommended Restaurants

In Mumbai, it's possible to eat well on a range of budgets. Even in a five-star restaurant, you'd be hard pushed to spend more than Rs1000 (£12.50/US\$22), while a filling meal in a *udipi* won't cost a tenth of that.

As a rule, run-of-the-mill restaurants frequented by Indian workers and tourists open early – by at least 8am – for fresh *idly-wada-chai-coffee* breakfasts; they then switch to *thalis (see page 98)* at lunchtime until 2.30–3pm, when afternoon snacks, such as *masala dosas* and *samosas*, are provided. More expensive restaurants open only for lunch (noon–3pm) and dinner (6.30–11pm). Indians tend to eat late, typically sitting down at 9pm – though, in the commercial districts such as Fort, restaurants fill up as soon as offices close at around 6pm. Sunday, when middle-class families often eat out, is the busiest day, and it's advisable to book a table if you want to go to an upscale restaurant. In fact, it's best to reserve ahead for any high-end establishment; phone numbers are given where this is recommended.

More restaurants are accepting payment by credit or debit card, but you should always check in advance. *Udipis* and snack joints only deal in cash. Bills may not include service charges *(see page 126)*.

\$\$\$\$\$	Rs1,000
\$\$\$\$	Rs500–1,000
\$\$\$	Rs300–500
\$\$	Rs100–300
\$	under Rs100

COLABA & KALA GHODA

All Stir Fry \$\$\$ *Gorden House Hotel, 5 Battery Street, Apollo Bunder, tel: 2287 1122.* Designer Oriental restaurant with sparse white decor and Chinese-style wooden benches. You pick your own ingredients and sauces, then watch them being wok-fried in showy style by the chefs.

Bade Miyan $ *Tulloch Road*. This kebab-*wallah*, who's been working from the same pavement behind the Taj for 30 years, is a Mumbai institution. Punters eat standing up, seated at rickety tables, or in their cars, with beers from the liquor store down the lane. Try the famous chicken tikka or sheesh kebab, rolled in hot *rotis*.

Busaba $$$$ *4 Mandlik Marg, tel: 2204 3779*. One of the city's hippest restaurants, serving sumptuous dishes from across Asia: Tibetan *momos*, Vietnamese fish sizzlers, or Korean glass noodle salad. DJs play on Fridays and Saturdays.

Café Samovar $$ *Jehangir Art Gallery, MG Road, tel: 2284 8000*. Artists, students and refugees from the stifling heat of the museum form the mainstay of this homely little café on a long, narrow garden verandah. Stuffed *parathas*, washed down with chilled guava juice or a cold Kingfisher beer, are a favourite. The café also offers main meals such as prawn curry and veg *dhansak*.

Indigo $$$$$ *4 Mandlik Marg, tel: 2236 8999*. South Mumbai's most fashionable place to eat, complete with valet parking and A-list celebs swanning in and out (the Clintons ate here once, and you can bank on spotting Bollywood stars most weekend evenings). For all that, a laid-back atmosphere prevails, and both the refined Indian fusion food and sophisticated decor warrant the hype.

Kailash Parbat $–$$ *1 Pasta Lane, near the Strand cinema*. 'KPs' is Colaba's best-loved snack and sweet joint, famous for its Sindhi *pakora* (vegetable chunks deep-fried in maize flour), *rasgulla* (sponge balls soaked in rose syrup) and yummy cashew-nut *barfi* (milk sweet). They also offer a full multi-cuisine menu, including all the usual delicious south Indian standards, across the street.

Kamat $ *sbs Marg (Colaba Causeway)*. Popular south Indian snack place on Colaba's main drag – a particularly good spot for fresh *idly-wada* breakfasts plus crunchy *masala dosas* throughout the day.

Khyber $$$$ *154 MG Road, Kala Ghoda, tel: 2267 3227*. Classic Moghul cuisine – from creamy *paneer shaslik* to melt-in-the-mouth chicken *makhanwalla* – served in suitably opulent surroundings. Waiters in black ties and paintings by some of India's best-known artists add to the sense of occasion. If you're pushing the boat out, go for the mixed kebab platter (available in veg or non-veg).

Konkan Café $$$$ *Taj President Hotel, Cuffe Parade, tel: 5665 0808.* Haute cuisine from coastal Maharashtra, Goa, Karnataka and Kerala at surprisingly restrained prices. Signature dishes include tiger prawn in sour *kokum* sauce, snappers steamed in banana leaves and divine pepper-garlic crab. The flavours are all painstakingly authentic and the service five-star.

Leopold's $$$ *SBS Marg (Colaba Causeway), tel: 2872 3362.* This old Parsi café, which opened in 1871 and has gone through many incarnations since, is where most foreign travellers spend time while in Mumbai, tucking into grilled sandwiches, pizzas and cold beers. Stick to the Western snacks and you won't go far wrong.

Olympia Coffee House $ *Rahim Mansion, 1 SBS Marg (Colaba Causeway).* For a taste of old Bombay, this wonderful old Muslim place, with its text-book 'Irani' decor, is a must. Settle down at one of the marble tables, and waiters in flowing salwar kameezes will bring you the famous house *biriyani* or *sheesh kebabs* with spicy yoghurt dips. There's a mezzanine floor 'for ladies'. No alcohol.

The Sea Lounge $$$ *Taj Mahal Hotel, Apollo Bunder.* Afternoon tea and cakes at a window seat in the Sea Lounge, overlooking the Gateway of India, is *de rigueur* for Raj-ophiles, and a good way for anyone not lucky enough to be staying at the Taj to sample its gentile charms.

FORT, CST (VT) & DHOBI TALAO

Apoorva $$ *Vasta House (Noble Chambers), SA Brelvi Road, tel: 2287 0335.* Sublime Konkan seafood – including what might well be the world's tastiest prawn *gassi* – served in a typically cramped 'Mangalorean' with low ceilings and tacky decor, just off Horniman Circle (look for the fairy lights wrapped around the tree). They also do a definitive Bombay duck, best enjoyed with steaming hot *appams* and cold beer. Just as good as Trishna *(see page 140)*, but at half the price.

Britannia $$ *Opposite the GPO, Sprott Road, Ballard Estate, tel: 2261 5264.* This dowdy old Irani restaurant commands a devoted following for its legendary *berry pulao*, made with chicken, mutton or vegetables sprinkled with piquant red berries that are still specially imported from Tehran. But be warned, the portions are gargantuan. Open lunchtimes only 11.30am–3.30pm.

Ideal Corner $$ *12 F/G Hornby View, Gunbow Street, tel: 2262 1930.* Renowned Parsi restaurant in the heart of Fort where the dishes remain as traditional as ever, despite a recent facelift. If they're offered, try *khichidi* prawn, lamb *dhansak* or the chicken *farsha*. And be sure to leave room for the quirky British-inflected house dessert, 'custard *lagan*'. Closed evenings and Sundays.

Jimmy Boy $$ *11 Bank Street, Vikas Building, off Horniman Circle, tel: 2270 0880.* There aren't many places left in Mumbai where non-Parsis can sample traditional Zoroastrian wedding food, but Jimmy Boy prides itself on keeping the traditions alive with its pomfret in green chilli sauce and mutton *pulao* with *dhansak* – though the atmosphere is decidedly Western.

Joshi Club $ *31-A Narottamwadi, Kalbadevi Road, tel: 2205 8089.* Gujaratis love wholesome, subtly flavoured vegetarian dishes made from elaborate blends of mild spices, and you're unlikely ever to come across a finer example than the *thali* served here – not that you'd guess it from the downbeat, grubby-walled dining hall. One of the city's gastronomic highlights, but hard to find – head north for 10 minutes up Kalbadevi Road from the Metro cinema on Dhobi Talao, and ask a local for '*Joshi bhonalaya*'.

Kyani's 'House of Cakes' Bakery $ *Opposite Metro cinema, Dhobi Talao.* The definitive old-school Irani café, verging on decrepit but still going strong on a diet of *bun maska* (essentially buttered white rolls) and biscuits dunked in fierce orange *chai*. Worth at least a pit stop en route to or from the nearby movie houses.

Mahesh Seafood Home $$$ *8-D Cowasji Patel Street, off PM Road, tel: 5695 5554.* This used to be the working man's Mangalorean, and though the decor and prices have gone decidedly up-market, the seafood's as good as ever. Try the stupendous *surmai* fry, or benchmark fish *gassi*.

Trishna $$$$ *7 Sai Baba Marg (Ropewalk Lane), Kala Ghoda, tel: 2270 1623.* Mumbai's most famous Mangalorean restaurant was the first to make 'coastal' (i.e. Konkan) cuisine famous in the city; Bollywood stars, cricket heroes and billionaires have all eaten here over the years – hence the over-the-top kitsch decor and sky-high prices. Pepper-garlic-crab is their signature dish, and it really is fantastic, but in truth you can eat just as well for a fraction of the cost at Apoorva *(see page 138)* or Mahesh *(see above)*.

Vithal Bhelwala $ *5 AK Naik Marg (Baston Road), close to CST (VT) Station.* Vithal Bhelwala is credited with inventing Mumbai's best-loved snack, *bhel puri*, and this is a safe, hygienic place to try it. There are 25 or more varieties on offer, along with other tasty nibbles such as samosas and *aloo tikki* (fried potato patties).

Yezdani's Bakery $ *11-A Cowasji Patel Road, Fort.* Among the few traditional Irani bakeries left in the Fort district. People from all over south Mumbai still order their Portuguese-style bread-roll 'buns' and flaky-pastry 'puffs' from here, along with wholegrain brown loaves and other new-fangled breads from the West. Step in to the worn wooden interior and ask the proprietor, the irascible Mr Zend M. Zend, for a piece of the famous Yezdani apple pie.

CHURCHGATE & NARIMAN POINT

Badshah Juice and Snack Bar $ *Opposite Crawford Market, Lokmanya Tilak Road.* Tall glasses of brightly coloured rose syrup and milk swimming with maize-flour vermicelli, *falooda* is the quintessential Mumbai soft drink, brought here by Irani Zoroastrians from Persia in the 1920s. This cramped little café opposite Crawford Market is its undisputed spiritual home. Royal *falooda* (basically 'the works') is the most popular choice, but they also do a delicious *kesar*-flavoured *falooda*, made with real saffron, as well as a range of fresh mango preparations, from pure juice to milk-shake, melba and *kulfi* (India's own sweet version of ice cream).

Cha Bar $$ *Oxford Bookstore, 3 Dinsha Vaccha Road, Church-gate.* Trendy bookshop café, frequented mostly by rich students from the university on the opposite side of the maidan, which offers teas from all over India (from disgusting Ladakhi yak-butter *chai* to more fragrant, fine-tipped Nilgiri). They also do a range of grilled sandwiches and other light meals and snacks. Open 10am–10pm.

Crystal $ *Chowpatty Seaface, near Wilson College.* Authentic Punjabi home cooking, dished up to mostly homesick north Indians in what must be the grimiest-looking restaurant on Back Bay – proof that appearances really can be deceptive. Because the vege-tarian food – *palak paneer* (spinach and soft cheese), *dal makhini* (black lentils in a creamy sauce) and *bhindi bhaji* (okra curry) – is unfailingly delicious and well worth the trip to Chowpatty.

Mocha Bar $$–$$$ *VN Road, tel: 5633 6070.* If you've ever want-ed to try a hookah pipe, this fashionable terrace bar on VN Road, decked out like a Turkish Queen's boudoir with carpets and bolster cushions, will satisfy your curiosity. That said, proper coffee, made on a proper coffee machine, is why most of its punters come here. Inside, the air-conditioned dining room offers more substantial Mediter-ranean *mezes* accompanied by pricey New World wines.

The Pearl of the Orient $$$$ *Ambassador Hotel, VN Road, tel: 2204 1131.* The regional Chinese food served in this four-star hotel's rooftop restaurant may not be as authentic, nor as inventive, as some of Colaba's pan-Asian places, but it really doesn't matter because the views over the city and Back Bay are astounding. Moreover, as the whole structure revolves 360° in an hour and a half, they change constantly. Arrive at least 30 minutes before sun-set. Reservation recommended.

The Tea Centre $$ *Resham Bhavan, 78 VN Road.* A cup of top-quality tea can be surprisingly hard to come by in Mumbai, but even aficionados should be impressed by some of the single-estate Assams, Darjeelings and Nilgiris on offer at this charming Raj-era establishment. A perfect place to catch your breath, only five minutes' walk from the seafront and tourist office.

SUBURBS

China Garden $$$$$ *Kemp's Corner, 250–550 August Kranti Marg, near Chowpatty Beach, tel: 2495 5589.* Owner-chef Nelson Wang only had Rs27 in his pocket when he arrived in Mumbai in the early 1980s. He's since become a multi-millionaire thanks to the reputation of his restaurant, the most authentic Chinese in the city and a much-loved haunt of the glam set. It's said there hasn't been an empty table here for over 11 years. Try the Mongolian Steamboat soup and famous Peking chicken. Reservations essential.

Haji Ali Juice Centre $ *Lala Lajpat Rai Road, Haji Ali Circle.* Situated just outside the entrance to Haji Ali's tomb, this place is famous across the city for its fresh pomegranate, *chickoo* (sapodilla), mango, orange and lychee juices, though they also offer *faloodas*, *lassis* and various milkshakes loaded with ice cream.

Mezzo Mezzo $$$$$ *JW Marriott Hotel, Juhu Tara Road, by Juhu Beach, tel: 5693 3000.* Home of Danio Galli, Mumbai's most celebrated Italian chef, who specialises in Tuscan and Sardinian cuisine. His menu changes every three months or so, but there are always succulent wood-fired pizzas on offer. Everything's imported fresh from Italy – hence the sky-high rates. A favourite of the glitterati, who then move on to the Enigma nightclub in the same hotel

Soul Fry $–$$$ *Silver Croft, Palli Malla Road, Bandra,* tel: 2604 6892. Traditional Konkani seafood, served in incongruously trendy surroundings, but at low rates (the taxi ride up here is likely to cost more than your bill). Come at lunchtime for the wonderful Goanstyle fish *thali*, comprising a couple of crisp-fried Bombay Ducks, slices of pomfret or *surmai*, spoonfuls of clams in coconut *masala*, *rotis*, *papads* and pickle, all for under Rs100. In the evenings, the pricier à la carte takes over. A lively bar serves beers and spirits.

INDEX